BANFF SPRINGS

THE STORY OF A HOTEL

BART ROBINSON

SUMMERTHOUGHT
BANFF, CANADA
1988

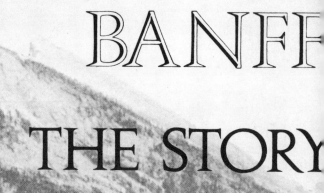

BANFF

THE STORY

SPRINGS

OF A HOTEL

Cover by Edward Goodall

Summerthought, Limited
Box 1420
Banff, Alberta

ISBN 0-919934-20-X

Printed and Bound in Canada by
Friesen Printers
a Division of D.W. Friesen & Sons Ltd.
Altona, Manitoba
Canada
R0G 0B0

Go, little book, God send thee good passage,
And specially let this be thy prayere
Unto them all that thee will read or hear,
Where thou are wrong, after their help to call
Thee to correct in any part or all.
—found in Karl Baedeker's
Handbook to Canada, 1907

Table of Contents

Introduction

"It had no business being there."

When Morley Roberts, an old railroad man, arrived in Banff in the summer of 1925 it had been 42 years since he'd visited the area. Things had changed.

Old man Goss, the fellow who ran the snake-bite-cure still on Whiskey Creek had long since disappeared, perhaps a victim of his own libations; the town was no longer CPR Siding 29, a random assortment of dusty shacks and tents at the foot of Cascade Mountain, but Banff, a bustling little alpine village which most immodestly claimed to be the centre of the greatest mountain playground on the continent, perhaps the world; and, most shocking of all, there was a castle rising majestically above the banks of the Bow River. The town was hard enough to accept, but Morley found a rock palace in the wilderness just a bit too much: "It had no business being there," he said, "for when I was thereabouts so long ago no one could have thought of it."

Morley visited and toured the anomaly—felt its walls, looked through its windows, talked to its inhabitants—and decided the building, like Banff, was a dream, and, like a dream, at once beautiful and absurd.

The castle, of course, was the Banff Springs Hotel and it was not a dream. But it was beautiful; and if it were absurd, well, there was a method in its madness.

Nor is the hotel today any less real than it was when Roberts visited the place—but many people who first visit the hotel today are overcome with the same emotions which Morley felt on his trip in 1925. The first-time visitor's inevitable questions are nearly programmed in their lack of variation: "What's *that*? What's it doing there? Who built it? Who owns it? Why? When? What for? How much?"

To start at the beginning, one must go back to the years just following Confederation and read the news about a struggling young company called the Canadian Pacific Railway.

I

William Van Horne
Capitalizes the Scenery

"Since we can't export the scenery, we'll have to import the tourists."

The Canadian Pacific Railway was never, by any normal standard, a modest child. Born the wealthy scion of economic necessity and political intrigue, two well-acquainted if not exactly well-respected bedfellows, its mere conception toppled John A. Macdonald's first government in 1873. And when, five years later, John A. was again in power and the unswaddled babe once more brought forth, it became cause for some of the greatest uproars ever known in an institution noted for great uproars. Words like "liar" and "coward" were bandied freely in the parliamentary chambers; and Liberal doomsayers, tongues clacking like Cassandra's, foresaw the day when the young company would become the proprietor of the government of Canada. But the Canadian Railway Bill, guaranteeing the company governmental support of 25 million dollars, 25 million acres of land, a 20-year monopoly of western trade, and freedom from taxes on all holdings in perpetuity, was passed by the Senate and became law February 15, 1881.

4

If the CPR were not a modest child, there was no reason it should have been, for railway building in Canada, as in Bismarck's Germany, Grant's America, and Cavour's Italy, was synonymous with nation building. The support the CPR received was an accurate reflection of the young country's impatience to get on with the achievement of the Victorian Age in Canada: the fulfillment of the pioneering myth—progress as measured by the replacement of wilderness by civilization. No one would deny a transcontinental railway would help tame the interior.

Politically, the railway was expected to tie up "the rags and ends of Confederation," British Columbia and the Maritimes; economically, it would give the tiring St. Lawrence commercial empire a bit of fresh blood and pry open the vast marketing possibilities of the Canadian interior. The CPR, in fact, promised its country even more: in an 1889 publication, *The New Highway to the Orient*, the company referred to itself as a young giant whose "arms at once reached out across that broad ocean and grasped the teas and silks of China and Japan to exchange for the fabrics of Europe and North America."

To make good its claim, the company faced the necessity of assuring more than a flow of grand words along the new tracks, and it was soon involved in the construction of facilities to feed and support the trains and their cargoes as they moved along the national artery. The dining pavilion was one such support, arising from an obvious need for passengers to retire for relaxation and refreshment from time to time along a rather tedious journey. From this elemental necessity the grandiose hotels of the CPR arose.

Such resting spots could have been quite simple structures—even shunted railway cars—and still fulfilled their purpose.[1] That they were not, and that they became instead internationally famous hotels, equated with royalty, representing the apex of elegant living, is due to the indefatigable energies of one man,

[1]As was the first such establishment at Rogers Pass. Such an arrangement, though, was only temporary in nature.

William Cornelius Van Horne. Formerly the general superintendent of the Chicago, Milwaukee, and St. Paul Railroad, Van Horne moved to Canada in 1882 to become general manager of the CPR. Within two years he had become vice-president of the line and had established himself as the "ablest railroad general in the world." Equally at home playing an all-night round of poker with railway navvies or examining some new addition to his world famous collection of Japanese porcelain, Van Horne wheeled his Brobdingnagian hulk from one end of the nation to the other, watching over his foundling line like a prairie hen watching over her brood.

Credit is given to Van Horne as the man who "capitalized the scenery" of the Canadian west. Tourism, he maintained, was one way of getting people to ride his line, and he was very aware of the dollar potential in the western mountain-scapes. Always a man to plunge to the heart of things, he summed up his philosophy succinctly: "Since we can't export the scenery," he said, "we'll have to import the tourists." Accordingly, with verve and dispatch, he launched a campaign to entice the *crème de la crème* of the international set (and anyone else with a bit of money) to the wilds of western Canada.

One of the cornerstones of the plan, the establishment of a system of luxurious hotels commanding the most scenic views of the Rocky and Selkirk Mountains, was the realization of one of Van Horne's most cherished dreams.[2] An amateur architect, he took great pleasure in sketching, modifying, and remodifying the designs for such structures. His goal was a series of lodgings to offer royal calibre guests all the comforts (at least) of home and still afford all the excitement of close wilderness contact. Who could resist? The promotion for the campaign painted a tantalizing, if perhaps somewhat exaggerated, picture:

May I not tempt you, kind reader, to leave England for a few short weeks and journey with

William Cornelius Van Horne, the "ablest railroad general in the world." "I eat all I can, I drink all I can, and I don't give a damn for anyone."

[2]Actually, the mountain hotels were only a part of a much larger system which Van Horne envisioned stretching from ocean to ocean.

me across that broad land, the beauties and glories of which have so recently been brought to within our reach? There will be no hardships to endure, no difficulties to overcome, and no dangers or annoyances whatever. You shall see mighty rivers, vast forests, boundless plains, stupendous mountains and wonders innumerable; and you shall see all in comfort, nay, in luxury.

With such luxurious accommodation in mind, the company undertook construction of three mountain hotels in 1886, less than a year after the driving of the last spike at Craigellachie. The Mount Stephen House at Field, the Fraser Canyon Hotel at North Bend, and the Glacier House at Rogers Pass, all in British Columbia, modelled to suggest Swiss chalets, rapidly became popular as alpine resorts. Glacier House in particular, at the heart of North America's "Little Switzerland," did such a booming business the CPR hired several Swiss mountain guides to live and guide climbs in the Rogers Pass area. Although the architect for the

Glacier House, Rogers Pass. Typical of the very earliest CPR mountain hotels, Glacier House was a very popular alpine resort at the turn of the century.

The earliest known rendering of the original Banff at the base of Cascade Mountain, painted in 1887 by the station agent, R. Clark.

first three chalets is not known, it's more than likely Van Horne played an important part in developing their common design: a three storey centre portion with two wings of different heights extending in opposite directions from the centre.

But these modest structures were merely appetizers for a man like Van Horne. While the first three hotels were being built he commissioned designs for another, larger, grander hotel to be constructed on the eastern slope of the Rockies at the confluence of the Spray and Bow Rivers in the newly established Rocky Mountain Park. Van Horne had taken the first decisive step toward the creation of the Banff Springs Hotel.

II

Château, Chalet?
Tudor, Gothic,
Renaissance?

"a few facts about the mammouth building
as being erected at Banff"

When Van Horne chose the confluence of the
Bow and the Spray as a hotel site, the nearby village
of Banff was not the sort of place a young man in
search of cosmopolitan fame and fortune would choose
to settle down.[1] Located about three miles north of the
present townsite, its amassed urban potential lay in just
over a dozen buildings: a few shacks, two hotels, three
stores and a livery stable. But if the town were a sleepy
little collection of rough-hewn buildings in the late

[1]One source, Robert Campbell, suggests that Van
Horne had originally planned to erect the hotel at
the foot of Tunnel Mountain, but that Tom Wilson,
a local packer and former guide to the railway during the survey, told Van Horne that he knew of a
better spot and took him to the place where the
Banff Springs now stands.

1880's, even then it held the germ which was to transfigure low log structures and muddy streets into one of the most famous mountain vacation spots in the world.

The combination of a Valkyrian backdrop and Sulphur Mountain's mineral hot springs, noted for their "great medicinal value," led Van Horne to endorse enthusiastically the proposal that the ten-square mile hot springs reserve (created in 1885 to prevent despoilation of the area), be made a national park in 1887.[2] With relatively easy access to the area provided by the railway it took no special divining of the augurers to foresee the small town's future. Indeed, the village received its first social recognition as early as '85 when it was named in honour of Lord Mount Stephen's native Banffshire, Scotland. (Lord Mount Stephen, George Stephen was president of the CPR from 1881 to 1888.) Siding 29, the earlier CPR cognomen, might have proved less difficult for future generations of tourists to pronounce, but it wasn't really a suitable name for an international resort.

Nor was the town to remain a dusty little mountain village for long. While cows strolled leisurely down the town's main street in the summer of '86, and the tourist's dollar was little more than a passing stroke of luck, things had happened in the east to mature a financial swan from an ugly duckling. Van Horne, it seems, had hired the architectural high priest of the Boston baronage, a man named Bruce Price, to design the Banff Springs Hotel.

Van Horne's attention may have been drawn to Price by the parlour cars he had designed for the Pennsylvania and Boston and Albany Railroad. It's just as likely, though, that Van Horne, an avid architectural neophyte, was familiar with the works of Price's teacher, Henry Hobson Richardson, one of the great names

Bruce Price, father of Emily Post and architect of the first Banff Springs Hotel.

[2]As early as 1883 Van Horne urged the creation of a national park at Lac des Arcs, an area some miles east of Banff. The Rocky Mountain Park, encompassing some 260 square miles surrounding the Banff hot springs, became Canada's first national park— "a public park and pleasure ground for the benefit, advantage and enjoyment of the people of Canada" —in 1887.

An early photograph of Banff Avenue, taken in the year 1887.

in American Victorian architecture. Price was commissioned by the CPR to design the new Windsor Station
in Montreal in 1886, and shortly thereafter was asked
to submit plans for the hotel at Banff.

With all the advantages of hindsight, we can
see that Price sired two noteworthy and enduring social
entities: Emily Post, the apostle of proper American
etiquette, was one; and the other, the "national style"
of architecture in Canada, that of the medieval French
château. One critic of Price's has stated that Emily's
"rationalization of anachronistic social behavior mir-
rored her father's ability to do the same for . . . architecture," but Price, despite his irregular reputation, is
without question one of the important men in the short
history of Canadian architecture.

At the time of Price's immigration in 1886,
Canadian builders were slowly developing the first
acceptable nationwide architectural mode, rooted firm-
ly in the British High Victorian Gothic revival. The

12

essence of Victorian architecture lay in the idea that any structure must have both architectural "reality" and "meaning." As Great Britain had settled upon the Gothic style, symbolic of a traditional past, for its favoured form, the assumption was the Dominion of Canada could do no better than adopt the ribbed vaulting, pointed arches, and flying buttresses of the Gothic for its central architectural motif as well. That it did occur is well evidenced by such structures as the Houses of Parliament at Ottawa and University College of Toronto, both structures of the 1850's.

By the 1880's, however, the central concept of architectural symbolism was beginning to be modified by two somewhat divergent trends which would have great bearing upon the future of North American architecture. One was "organicism," the idea that a building should be a natural, organic extension of the surrounding environment. The other was the "Beaux-Arts" movement, based on the idea that "reality" in architecture could best be expressed through the precedents of the past made bigger and better with the technologies and materials of the present.

Price, although he won his reputation as a master of the "Beaux-Arts," was very much aware of both of the newer trends, as well as having a fine feeling for "good old fashioned" architectural symbolism. Indeed, in the sixteenth-century châteaux of the Loire he found a style he thought could combine all three: the symbol, the architectural reality, and an architectural mode which he felt befitted organically the harsh Canadian environment. More than one present day architectural historian has stated that Price's structures were more archaeologically than organically oriented, that they were built more to convey the idea of luxury at the expense of the environment, but Price, at least, believed his edifices to be concerned with both. The châteaux of the Loire, characterized by massive wall surfaces which were flat and crisp, steep roofs, a central tower, and round turrets flanking the doors, he thought were quite appropriate for the northern climate, and most suitable for the mountainous regions. As for improving on the style of the past, Price was pleased to note in an 1899 architectural periodical that he had "had the entire resources of the Canadian Paci-

"There is a large class of buildings erected by Mr. Price in which the French architecture of the early part of the XVI century has been used with great freedom and intelligence. . . ."
Russell Sturgis, 1899

*Bruce Price's original sketch for the CPR Hotel at Banff. The
completed hotel differed from the sketch only in that it lacked
the pyramidal portion of the roof.*

fic Railway to draw upon, and hence it was possible to
build with certain materials in certain ways."

Whether Price's buildings were architectur-
ally organic, or archaeological, or symbolic, they did
exhibit the important features of Late Victorian architecture: they were visually clean and attractive, pleas-
ing in line and colour, well adapted to a picturesque
site, and without exception capable of exciting all but
the very dullest of imaginations. The style, in fact,
proved so exciting, so "very right" for Canada, that it
became the focal point of Canadian architecture, and
Price, unwittingly, became the father figure of a style
which remained vigorous until the start of the second
world war. Indeed, so influential was the château style
that throughout the early 1900's it was the only architectural mode acceptable for government structures.
Price's own Canadian works include the Windsor Station, the Place Viger Hotel and Station, the Château
Frontenac (interestingly enough, said to be modelled
after H. H. Richardson's lunatic asylum in Buffalo,
New York—obviously a versatile design) and, of course,
the early Banff Springs Hotel.

Although there is little information concerning the cost or actual construction of the first Banff

"Whatever is picturesque in
a design should be accom-
plished by the exigencies of
the site rather than
deliberately made. . . . A
truly picturesque effect can
never be produced
deliberately. . . . It can only
be had by adding part to
part without deliberate
design or intent."
—Bruce Price, 1899

Springs, it would appear that work on the foundations commenced as early as the fall of 1886, the same year the plans were commissioned. The labour for the job was undoubtedly supplied by a crew of CPR construction workers, many of them Chinese, brought to Banff specifically to work on the hotel, as the local labour force at that time would not have exceeded sixty to seventy men.

Despite the shortage of actual construction detail, there does exist, mainly in old newspapers, a certain amount of more general information about the proposed hotel. As any event involving a high degree of imagination and boldness, or great amounts of capital, will engage the public's curiosity, so the idea of the Banff Springs Hotel caught the fancy of a certain portion of the Canadian public; and people across the nation were interested in news concerning this tribute to elegance under construction in a region which seemed as coarse and unsettled as the image of the country itself.

An article in the *Winnipeg Sun*, dated 1887 and entitled "The Great Hotel: A few facts About the Mammouth Building as Being Erected at Banff," gave Manitobans the latest information on the building, the word coming directly from CPR General Superintendent Whyte, who was carrying the plans for the hotel from Montreal to Banff:

> The hotel, which will be built by the company, the work being done under the supervision of their own officials, is to be a mammouth affair, and to contain 250 beds. It is to be constructed entirely of timber, three stories in height with a dormer in the roof, and a basement excavated in rock; it will be in two main wings, the front being the largest, and this will contain a rotunda, rising to the height of the building, and an elevator. The rear wing will be devoted mainly to the commissariat and domestic apartments. The hotel will have its own gas and water works, and also be supplied with electric lights and electric appliances.

In architectural fact, the building emerged a somewhat different creature from the one for

One of the earliest photographs of the Banff Springs, taken about 1888.

which General Superintendent Whyte carried blueprints across the nation. No one seems to remember
the name of, or even admit knowledge of, the CPR
official who was in charge of the construction, but it
is well-known and recorded that when Van Horne
cheerily eased his girth into Banff in the summer of
1887, he found the rapidly rising hotel turned 180°
from what the plans called for. This had the somewhat
disastrous effect of affording the kitchen staff the "mil-
lion-dollar view" of the confluence of the Bow and the
Spray, and left the guests in their rotunda viewing the
pine trees on the flanks of Sulphur Mountain. Van
Horne was not amused. As one of his colleagues stated,
"Van Horne was one of the most considerate and even-
tempered of men, but when an explosion came it was
magnificent." However, even in its most explosive
moments, Van Horne's mind continued to function

Van Horne's CPR station at Banff, reputedly designed on a piece of scrap paper in a matter of minutes.

smoothly and deliberately, and by the time the reverberations of his voice had echoed into the further reaches of the Bow Valley, he had sketched a rotunda pavilion and ordered that it be built behind the kitchen, thus resurrecting the coveted view.

Van Horne's architectural acumen and legendary speed of response were illustrated again a bit later when someone asked about plans for a new CPR station in Banff. Van Horne reputedly snatched up a piece of brown paper, sketched in a few hurried lines, and handed it back to the inquirer: "Lots of good logs there. Cut them, peel them, and build your station."

In spite of misread blueprints and any of the lesser catastrophes which seem to be an inherent risk in any large construction job, work on the hotel proceeded rapidly, and by the early spring of 1888 the building was nearing completion. The structure, as

Dave White and Bill Peyto at the Banff Station about the turn of the century.

early accounts and photographs portray it, was a four-storey (three main storeys and a dormered roof) frame building, resembling in shape the letter "H," the two wings forming the vertical members of the letter. Van Horne's pavilion jutted out toward the river from the front wing. The exterior was veneered to suggest cream-coloured Winnipeg brick, trimmed with oil-finished cedar shingles from British Columbia. The romantic medieval air of the building was accentuated by the steep-hipped roofs with pointed, finialed dormers, corner turrets, and large oriels.

Debates about the stylistic sources of the building raged. One traveller referred to its being "in the Schloss style of the Rhenish provinces," while another believed it to be "something like a wooden combination of the Tudor hall and Swiss chalet." Yet another was correct in assuming the French château as the hotel's inspiration, but then went on to surmise that it was built "as a gesture of recognition to the French-Canadian population and in tribute to the French explorers

oriel: a large window built out from a wall and resting on a bracket or corbel.

finial: an ornament at the top of a spire, gable, etc.

Dormer: a window set upright in a sloping roof.

who had blazed the trail for the Canadian Pacific," a thought which, although plausible, probably never entered Price's head.

But if the hotel were loose stylistically, it was indeed picturesque, and there was little argument about its uniqueness. (Actually, Price and his successors to the CPR château tradition became stylistically more concise in the buildings of later years, including the present Banff Springs Hotel, but it could never be said that any of the CPR architects was chained to the concept of exact archaeological reproduction.)

And if the exterior of the building were exciting, the interior was at least visually piquant. Finished in native pine and fir, the inside area was dominated by a huge glass-covered octagonal rotunda which served as the main lobby of the building. The upper floors of the structure opened onto the central hall in balconies in successive galleries, making it possible for the guests to leave their bedrooms "and gape down at the company assembled there." A large reading room, various parlours, dining rooms, smoking rooms, offices and a few guest rooms occupied any ground floor not taken by the central rotunda, while most of the area in the upper two storeys was devoted to guest accommodation, many of the rooms being *en suite*.

The basement held, other than the machinery for the electric lights, promise for the gentlemen guests who tired of the mountain scenery and perhaps their wives: a fine bar and billiard room offered a dignified retreat. A separate building housed boilers for steam heat and a large bathhouse, the latter supplied with the mineral waters of the sulphur hot springs which were piped down the mountainside and into the ten separate bathing rooms and the common plunge.

Such, then, was the state of the Banff Springs Hotel when it first opened its doors in the spring of 1888.

III

Vistas and Vendettas:
The Hotel in the '90's

"the dining room is not so good; being
reminiscent of an Italian convent being
turned into a barrack."

While many of the early guests of the Banff
Springs Hotel might have taken issue with Van Horne's
proclamation that it was the "Finest Hotel on the
North American Continent," few would argue about
the atmosphere encountered there. An air of rarefied
extravagance permeated the building, percolating up
through the exclusive French service in the dining
room, spilling over into the plush comforts of the
smoking and reading rooms.

Van Horne and Price set out to create a very
specific type of milieu by constructing an edifice adorn-
ed with all the accoutrements of a romantic past, and
in their task they succeeded splendidly. "Did it matter,"
asks one historian, speaking of the early CPR château
hotels in general, "if their size disguised a fundamental
formlessness, their exotic detail was meaningless, their
treatment of materials and plan monotonous and arti-
ficial?" Not at all—so long as the hotels fulfilled their
function and their symbol: a pleasant presentation of

refined romantic elegance. If the guests couldn't quite put their collective finger on the archaeological origin of the Banff Springs, they could make their conjectures in a very clean and well-lighted place.

The significance of the hotel, however, did not cease with the establishment of a graciously hedonistic aura for the individual guests. With the other CPR hotels it played an important social role for the wealthier members of Canadian society, filling in the cultural vacuum which was found on the western side of the Atlantic.[1] Capitalism, *laissez faire*, and the lack of a federal income tax combined to create great personal fortunes both in Canada and the United States, and the young empire-builders were determined to prove themselves worthy of their new-found wealth. For these people the hotels presented a chance "to pose in the elegant costume of an age of social class, which suggested that those who entered the ballrooms of the place were invited guests of rank, gentlemen and ladies of importance, squires rather than peasants." And for the Europeans of established wealth the hotels were a demonstration that Canada was not wanting in proper cultural decorum.

Whatever its social province, the hotel was an impressive structure, "a stately pile," as one budding journalist put it, and it never failed to draw inspired dithyrambs, however contrived, from first visitors. The quaint but most enlightening Victorian institution, the published travel journal, has fortunately preserved many of these accolades, and a random sampling establishes that the hotel was "comfortable and daring," "one of the finest structures of its kind in Canada," "a most sumptuous affair, as palatial as a Monterey or Saratoga hotel," "a wonder of art and invention in the wilderness," and finally, even to outdo Van Horne's own edict, "the best mountain hotel in the world."

The guests who held such opinions were a varied lot, but all found common denominators in possessing a fair amount of money and in coming to the

[1]By 1900 the CPR had hotels in Montreal (Place Viger Hotel and station), Quebec City (Château Frontenac), and Vancouver (Hotel Vancouver), as well as Banff, Lake Louise, Field, North Bend, and Rogers Pass.

hotel via the railroad. Staying at the hotel was rarely an end in itself (at least in the earliest years of its existence) but rather was one of several stops on a long and arduous, albeit exciting, transcontinental journey, undertaken as either a vacation or, equally likely, as the shortest and most efficient route to the Orient from Europe. Taking such a trip was a popular if expensive thing to do, and the idea appealed to Europeans with hereditary wealth, to the robber barons and the *nouveaux riches* of America, to princes, to politicians, to patrons of the arts, even to the dour financiers of eastern Canada.

Along the way one could be assured of exchanging pleasantries and practising one-upmanships with the "proper" people, and it was to this end the hotel played its full hand. As one early visitor to Banff so ably put it:

> One who stays here for two hours realizes the distinction between "the man who lived in the terraced house and the brother in the streets below" . . . for one either stops at *The Hotel*, or he does not. . . . There are several hotels—some on hillsides set in pleasant parks, others on the banks of the Bow River, and some on the main street of town—and then there is the Banff Springs Hotel. . . .

The idea that the Banff Springs was *The Hotel* began as soon as the guest alighted from his coach on the Imperial Limited onto the long wooden boardwalk of the Banff Station and was confronted by a long line of hack drivers and employees of the various hotels in town, each shouting out the name and virtues of his particular establishment. The din of the rival voices might at first give the traveller the impression that Banff was a large and cosmopolitan metropolis with the greatest array of deluxe accommodation on the continent. But it didn't take too long to sort out the confusion and realize that the tallyho of the Banff Springs Hotel, by virtue of its size, platform position, and well-groomed team of either four or six horses, was the obvious choice for those who were serious about their pleasures.

Tallyho: A large horse-drawn omnibus, capable of carrying up to sixteen persons. It derives its name from its British birthplace, where a trumpeter would always sit next to the driver and announce the coach's arrival with a great fanfare.

A twenty-minute ride on the tallyho carried the guests from the station to the great arcade of the hotel's courtyard, where visitors arriving by day caught their first glimpse of the busy life implicit in a mountain resort:

> In the courtyard are riding-horses and grooms in cowboy costumes, smoothly tailored women about to go for a climb in the mountains, and uniformed servants standing at the entrance eager to be of assistance to arriving or parting guests. It is a picture that one imagines exists only in reality at some medieval castle in Tyrol.

Complementary colours and images followed the guests inside the building, where they found all the latest conveniences, including electric lights, steam heat, and even an elevator for those too infirm or too dignified to climb two flights of stairs. The visitors would pay $3.50 *per diem* and this, at twice the expense of the other hotels in town, would provide "a luxuriously furnished room, a private bath, and fare much the same as on an Atlantic liner," everything, in fact, but the wine.

One malcontent found the main dining room "not so good," reminiscent, indeed, "of an Italian convent . . . turned into a barrack," but there were always those smoothly-tailored women and live chamber music to dispel further thoughts of regimentalization, sacred or martial.

"We tried both principal hotels, the Canadian Pacific and the Sanitarium; the former cost nearly double as much as the latter, but then it is a palace hotel. . . ."
—Douglas Sladen, 1895

> You sit at dinner in style, and eat your fried chicken *à la* Maryland to the "March El Capitan" or a *Fantaisie* from *Der Freischütz*, played by the Melrose Trio—three clever young ladies who are great on the piano, the violin, and the seductive 'cello'. You look out on the mountains from any or every window, and are fetched back from a reverie by an American female at your table ordering green tea.

The musicians would also present concerts of serious music each evening after dinner, invariably causing the young to sentimentalize and the old to become retrospective.

Other favourite after-dinner pastimes included a session in the bar and billiard room where the affairs of the world—the discovery of gold in the Yukon, Laurier's new Liberal government, and the threat of colonial war in South Africa—might be put in order any number of times; a moonlight stroll down to the Bow Falls; and, for the European guests, chatting with an American couple, a constant source of delight and amazement for the travel journal set. The combination of American innocence and money proved irresistible for many of the British guests. As one visitor summed it up:

> Some of [the Americans] are very plain people, and tell the story of how they became rich with much *naïveté*, disowning the idea of their possessing any special faculty (in which the hearer is disposed to agree with them) and confessing also that they don't know what to do with their money now they've got it, which also seems easily understandable.

Another guest relates the experience of watching a group of new arrivals from the States look on in wonderment as the British guests stand for the band's ten p.m. rendition of "God Save the Queen."

> 'Wall,' said one lady to another while waiting for the lift. 'I think it was jest sweet of them Britishers. I've come into a foreign country, long ways from home, and they played the American tune, "My country 'tis of Thee," and all the Britishers stood. I cud hev jest cried with happiness!'

"Some of us," says the raconteur, "jest smiled."

It would, of course, be wrong to assume that all the early guests were either stuffy Englishmen out to sharpen up their *noblesse oblige* or ingenuous Americans out to reveal their ignorance. One of the early frequenters of the hotel who managed to avoid both vices was none other than Lady Agnes Macdonald, the wife of Canada's first Prime Minister, a highly energetic woman who posssessed a rare combination of cultural propriety and a taste for such earthy pleasures as riding on the cowcatchers of locomotives.[2]

> [2]Her record distance for such a feat seems to have occurred in 1886 when she rode the 'catcher most of the distance from Laggan (Lake Louise) to Vancouver, nearly 600 miles, even though her husband dismissed the whole affair as "rather ridiculous."

She became so enamoured of Banff during an 1886 transcontinental trip that she had a private cottage built for her adjacent to the hotel. The cottage was used by Lady Macdonald during the summers of '87, '88, and '89 (and thus she would have watched the hotel being built). She combined her love for word games and her hobby of woodcarving by inscribing *If the B m.t. put : it,* above the fireplace.[3] The cabin, known as the Earnscliffe cottage, still stands today, located a short distance south of the upper staff annex. Since Lady Macdonald's time the cottage has been used as a residence for both hotel managers and hotel staff, a storage room, and a rental shop for snowmobiles. Recent developments, however, call for restoration of the cottage as a guest house.

Another early frequenter of the hotel, the nephew of Lord Mount Stephen, was as interesting as Lady Macdonald, if for slightly different reasons. He disliked hotel lobbies as much as Lady Agnes liked cowcatchers. He took all his meals in his room and used the room's window as entrance and exit for his chambers, preferring never to cross through the rotunda and use the hotel's main doors.

Lord Mount Stephen's nephew: early and eccentric.

Another early guest of note, a bit more sociable, was a young, good-looking millionaire named Ross Thompson, the avatar in that western rags-to-riches myth wherein the very amiable but very broke young cowpuncher invests his last twenty dollars in two uncertain mine claims and comes through with the mother lode. Which is precisely what happened to Thompson in 1895; and in the summer of 1896, both his fortune and his reputation established, he checked into the Banff Springs Hotel, more than ready to mix a little business with his pleasure.

It seems that Thompson had been in Banff before, during the spring of 1895, bumming a train ride toward the British Columbia interior and his fortune, and he had been arrested and run out of town for vagrancy. Now, a year later, he was back, but this time he travelled first class. It was doubly a pleasure to be

[3]Translated, the inscription reads, "If the grate be empty, put coal on it."

A stroll to the Bow Falls proved a popular excursion with early hotel guests.

"He will be sure to feel a strong desire to ascend some of the heights, and to gain varied and closer views of many points of scenery that will especially interest him. He will, of course, want to visit the various springs, to cross the Spray, and to walk down the Bow until he can look backward between Tunnel and Rundle Mountains; he will want to study the falls from every accessible point of view, and, taking the little steamer or a canoe, ascend the Bow, push his way into the Vermillion Lakes, and construct for himself varied pictures of the mountains. . . ."
—Bernard McEvoy, 1902

back in town when he discovered that a man by the name of Stellarton was registered at the hotel. Stellarton was one of a group of New York financiers who had tried unsuccessfully to separate Thompson from his mines earlier in the year. Stellarton, aspiring to the select social circle of the "New York 400," was eager to meet Thompson and set things straight—and introduce Thompson to his daughter.

During his week at the hotel Thompson made himself pleasantly available to the other guests, struck up friendships with many of the townspeople, innocently courted Stellarton's daughter, and became friendly with Inspector Harper of the Royal Northwest Mounted Police. He was, he said, interested in police work.

On his final night in Banff, Thompson graciously invited the Stellarton family and Inspector Harper to a private dinner party where he wined and dined them most elegantly. Arrangements with the head waiter called for full glasses at all times; and while Thompson talked much and sipped little, his guests talked little and drank much. The end of the evening saw poor Mrs. Stellarton first under the table and then being carried to her room by Thompson and Manager Mathews, with Harper and Mr. Stellarton not far behind, arm-in-arm, vociferously discussing the possibilities of a national police force for the U.S.A., Inspector Harper, of course, heading up the whole show. A bit later, when Harper was finally loaded into the buggy waiting to carry him back to the barracks, the driver, a corporal in the force, was asked to remind Harper to glance over the police record for June 17, 1895, when he awoke the next morning.

Within a day the news of the dinner had spread throughout the hotel and the town—the Stellartons judiciously decided that perhaps they would spend the rest of their vacation in a spot where the snickers (many of them from behind the cuffs of the "400") weren't quite so pointed, and Inspector Harper, one would assume, wished he might do the same.

Although there were no doubt other intrigues hatched in the hotel, the major business of the hotel was simply recreation and pleasure.[4] Thompson to the contrary, it was highly unlikely that the guest of the 1890's or early 1900's would run afoul of an industrious drummer or high-pressure salesman "with a scheme on." The only real business was to stretch the body and spirit in the mountain sunshine and listen to the humming of one's own head in a wilderness silence which had yet to be broken by the racket of an "infernal" combustion engine.

It was, in fact, the wilderness environment which provided much of the uniqueness of the hotel,

[4]Hotels, and particularly hotels associated with mineral baths, occupy an interesting and important position in the history of political and military intrigue. The great spas of Europe, Baden-Baden and the baths at Ems, were the sites of many crucial political meetings from the 16th to 19th century. Banff, of course, is central only to itself and was fortunately separated in both time and space from the great affairs of Europe. Some would even say North America.

A pack train prepares for departure from the Banff Springs Hotel courtyard, circa 1903.

setting it quite apart from its more civilized counterparts further to the east. For while it was possible to listen to Lizst's *Second Rhapsodie* on a new Steinway in the evening ("a treat hardly to be expected in the middle of the Rockies"), the daytime hours presented a somewhat different face, a mad swirl of earthy outdoor activity. Packers like Tom Wilson and George Fear and James Brewster dated their businesses to the first years of the hotel; and the era of men like Bill Peyto (who reputedly had eyes so fierce and piercing they'd make a grizzly bear back down a trail) and James Simpson (who was to become the "grand old man of the mountains" in later years) was close at hand. The CPR-imported Swiss guides were never far away, ever-ready to find mountains worthy of the guests' alpenstocks. All in all, the various mountain men and the exotic paraphernalia of their respective trades marked a colourful and highly stimulating contrast to the world of crinolines and spats, and most of the guests were willing to exchange the formality of eastern dress for a pair of sheepskin chaps or a pair of tricouni-nailed climbing boots.

A winter sleigh ride at the Banff Springs, 1896. Manager Mathews in the back seat.

Hiking, canoeing, taking a pleasure cruise up the Bow on the "Mountain Belle," or renting "bronchoes" or a tallyho for a ride out to the Hoodoos or Devil's Lake (Lake Minnewanka) were favourite pastimes. Fishing was an openly competitive event, the guests vying with each other for the greatest poundage —a competition which once went so far as to see one party stuff its best effort with ten pounds of rocks, a ploy discovered and decried back at the hotel when some impudent non-competitor dared to observe that the fish's mouth had been sewn shut!

Yet another sort of sport was offered by the many virgin peaks of the Rockies themselves, and many famous European climbers were enticed to the Banff vicinity and the hotel by the rumour of untrod summits. Finding the number of unclimbed mountains in the Alps rapidly diminishing, men like James Outram and Arnold Mumm were drawn to western Canada by the thought of whole ranges of mountains which were yet to be named, let alone climbed. Edward Whymper, conqueror of the Matterhorn and one of the élite of the Alpine Club, organized his first outing in the Rockies at the Banff Springs Hotel, although with some difficulty for he viewed the local packers as some sort of sub-species. It was only after Manager Mathews took him aside and patiently explained that Canadians, too, believed themselves to be real people that Whymper humbled himself enough to engage Bill Peyto as a guide and packer for his first trip.

In speaking of entertainments, not to be forgotten are the hot springs, "hot sulphurous water gushing from the earth for the hypochondriacs to drink, and the halt, lame, and withered to bathe in as well." Actually, the springs proved popular with all the guests whether they needed brimstone or not, although it is true that the major publicity drive was directed toward the waters' curative powers, they being "especially efficacious for the cure of rheumatic, gouty, and allied conditions," as well as for conditions of "the liver, diabetes, Bright's disease and chronic dyspepsia." The water was piped down to the hotel from the Upper Hot Springs, located some 800 feet above the hotel on the side of Sulphur Mountain. Various plumbing problems often resulted in such a reduced flow of water that little if any reached the hotel's pool, and at such embarrassing times the hotel staff would surreptitiously fill the pool with hot water and dump in bags of sulphur, a ploy which worked tolerably well until the water was again arriving from the springs proper.

"The only business at Banff is to enjoy one's self, to recreate, to loaf in the sunshine and worship nature."
—Bernard McEvoy, 1902

There was, it appears, no lack of things to do, either at the hotel or in its immediate environs. Although the Banff Springs can't claim any such bear stories as the one boasted by Dr. Brett's Sanitarium Hotel, which centred around Sergeant Casey Oliver's pet bear wandering into the hotel one night and deciding to climb into bed with one of the unsuspecting guests, it could never be said that any early Banff Springs visitor ever died of boredom.

IV

Banff's Bread and Butter
The Halt,
Lame, and Withered

*"more destitute of bird and beast and flower
than a Park at Montreal"*

The hotel and its traffic were bound to have
an effect on "the man in the streets below," and the
little town of Banff was as quick to capitalize the tourist as Van Horne had been to capitalize the scenery. By
1900 the village had managed to transport itself from
the foot of Cascade Mountain to the foot of Tunnel
Mountain, and small shops, restaurants, and new hotels
leapt forth from the wilderness to create a bustling
Banff Avenue. Guides and packers found the area lucrative; and someone, after all, had to provide services for
those "halt, lame, and withered," that came to cast
aside their crutches at the various hot springs establish-
ments. The Banff Springs, the largest hotel and entertaining the wealthiest clientèle, and having the resources
of the CPR to back any innovations to bring yet more
people to the area, played a rather critical role in the

Banff economy. "The Banff Springs," one resident has unromantically reminisced, "was Banff's bread and butter."

The town grew rapidly (considering its diminutive population when it found itself the seat of a national park in 1887) and most visitors discovered the townspeople to be a congenial sort, although there are reports the business community was inclined to be a bit overly-concerned with its own importance, something not too alarming since such concern seems to be the nature of business communities everywhere. It's probably true, though, that one of the travel journal set was being a bit callous when he wrote in 1895 that:

> Not that the town of Banff has much to boast of. It has a few hundred inhabitants, who have succeeded in making the surrounding woods and mountains more destitute of bird and beast and flower than a Park at Montreal. Though it consists of but a single street, it is horribly over-civilized. It has even a chemist, from whom, as far back as three or four years ago, you could buy Kipling's books in the unauthorised editions published by the Harpers.

Destitution, over-civilization, and Kipling's books to the contrary, the town seems to have had a good heart— young Ross Thompson, on his first unfortunate journey through Banff, was given a gift of cheese and bread, no questions asked, by an old French grocer. The act, incidentally, was not forgotten by Thompson on his second journey to town—on that occasion he managed to visit "Frenchy" once each day, buying a bit of candy for the grocer's children and paying for it with a five-dollar gold piece.

The town was able to overlook most aspersions cast its way from the "castle on the hill." In later years the hotel's "snob element" would rankle some of the community's aspiring socialites just as surely as the hotel's platform privileges at the CPR station would rankle other hotel owners, but there was certainly no such gulf in the first two decades of the hotel's existence. The town managed to maintain a pride in the hotel that bordered on boosterism, and an article in an early issue of the local paper, after describing the beauties of the building, goes so far as to grant it immunity from the world of finance:

It does no[t] seem fit that one should go into detail on the money or the toil it has cost to bring this incomparable institution to its present stage of perfection. Mercenary ideas jar the romance of the situation.

Despite the town's pride in the hotel, as well as its dependence upon the hotel for a certain portion of its meal ticket, few of the townspeople ever saw the inside of the hotel, and most were only vaguely aware of the elegant activities which transpired behind the great carved doors. It was very much "a palace unto itself," and very few of the local populace would consider directly transgressing its glittering domain. The concept of social class was a very vigorous doctrine at the turn of the century and it operated most effectively to keep the "downtown people" downtown.

Yet there were some annual events which tended to bring the hotel and the town into contact with each other on a social plane. The annual hotel summer ball carried the established families of Banff and Calgary briefly into the sequestered realm of the

New York and Boston social registers, and lucky guests of the occasions could later speak in casual tones of mingling with European and Eastern royalty.

Another event, this one for all comers, was the Banff Indian Days, a mid-summer ritual which has continued to this day. The whole thing began in 1889[1] when an extended period of bad weather washed out several CPR bridges in British Columbia and all train traffic was halted. Manager Mathews, trying to think up new entertainments for his marooned guests, called on Tom Wilson to round up some local Indians, members of the Stony tribe, to dance for the guests. The impromptu activity proved so popular with both the hotel visitors and the townsfolk that it became an annual affair.

There were other items, a bit more mundane, which helped to keep the hotel and town in touch. Many of the staff and labourers at the hotel were of Chinese ancestry, and if a few of the guests at the hotel wished to make a class distinction between themselves and the people of Banff, the people of Banff were certainly not above making a distinction between themselves and the Chinese workmen—God knows whom the Chinese found to pick on. A local news item dated 1903 reports that:

> The Chinamen who are working on the Banff Springs Hotel had trouble and bloodshed among themselves yesterday afternoon. A dispute over a fan tan game on the night previous was the cause of the row. When the first blows were exchanged the tribe split into sections and there was a general rush to arms, mop handles being the popular weapon. Ah Bing landed a knockout on Sing Some, while One Lung was sent to the floor under the mop handle of Fun Soon. Yip Bang and Look Sick with a space of fifteen feet between them performed threatening gymnastics and dodged imaginary uppercuts. The other belligerents made faces at each other.

[1]There is some controversy as to the exact year of the first Indian Days. Various sources favour different dates, the earliest being 1889, the latest, 1899.

"Old Jim Stink," one of the early Chinese labourers in Banff.

The same paper calmly editorializes that "we would not deprive the Chinamen of a living, but we would rather he make it in some place outside of Banff, four or five thousand miles away if convenient." The theme was recurrent throughout the following decade.

Another common problem which troubled both Banff and the hotel was that of the indigent transient, a problem which has plagued the better sensibilities of Banff since before the turn of the century. The transient of 1900 took one of two forms: the common hobo, also known as the boxcar bum (Ross Thompson would have fallen into this category on his 1895 sojourn), or the gentleman thief, the man who would ride the train legitimately in order to strike up an acquaintance with wealthy travellers and then steal as much of whatever was convenient at the first possible chance.

Both types were anathema to the town. An early news article entitled "The Tramp Nuisance Infesting our Mountain Resorts," decries the presence of such men in Banff: "They must be taught that these sylvan retreats, though free to the world, must be kept absolutely free if not from their presence at any rate from their outrages." At one point the possibility of gentlemen thieves operating at the Banff Springs forced Manager Mathews to ask guests to be most particular with the disposition of their possessions. Both the man in the terraced house and his brother in the streets below discovered that irritation, like love, was a common itch.

V

Growing Pains
and Capital Gains

*"the record of meals served per month
at the hotel has exceeded by 2000 the figure
of the great Seattle fair season of two years ago."*

By the beginning of the twentieth century it was apparent that Van Horne's scheme for a series of mountain hostels had been a stroke of genius. Within twelve years of its opening, the Banff Springs Hotel had become one of the top two or three mountain resorts on the North American continent, had established a solid international reputation for itself, and was proving to be a lucrative venture for the Canadian Pacific Railway.[1] The scenery had indeed been capitalized.

[1] The Banff Springs was, in fact, famous as a hotel regardless of the mountains. The *Baedeker Guide to Canada*, published in 1894, listed it as one of the top five hotels in the Dominion. The other four were the Château Frontenac in Quebec, the Windsor Station in Montreal, and the Russell House and Grand Union in Ottawa. The Banff Springs was particularly noted for its "good cuisine and attendence."

Van Horne had stepped up to the position of the chairman of the board (the company's presidency was now held by Thomas Shaughnessy), and it must have been at least a small source of pride for the man to see requests for hotel additions and improvements flow across the large, polished oak desks of the company's headquarters in Montreal.

Such requests were not a small matter. The hotels, in relation to the number of visitors requiring their services, were shrinking every year. The Banff Springs in particular was experiencing the most severe cramping. The Rocky Mountain Park superintendent's reports to Ottawa for the years 1902-05 reveal the demands with which the hotel was trying to cope: in 1902 hotel guests numbered 3,890; the following year the number of visitors reached 5,303; and in 1904 the number jumped to 9,684! The reports also indicate that during each of those years large numbers of guests were turned away for lack of accommodation.

The Banff Springs Register, which the park superintendent considered some of the best reading material in Banff in 1905, showed on one page names from South Africa, the Hague, Paris, Austria, England, Japan, Canada, the U.S., Borneo and Hong Kong.

In order to meet the demands of an expanding international clientèle, the CPR started a programme of hotel extension and improvement which fostered an addition or rearrangement in the Banff Springs' structure almost every year between 1900 and 1928, the year in which the present hotel was completed. The 28-year span is neatly divided into two periods: 1900 to 1910, during which all modifications dealt directly with the original 1888 building, and 1910-1928, during which all modifications were directed toward the ultimate end of a "new" hotel.

Exact dates and figures concerning construction at the Banff Springs from 1900 (and before) to 1910 are few and far between. The superintendent's reports comment that large additions were made in 1903, 1904, and 1905. Of these additions the most extensive was that of the winter of 1902-03. In 1902 the CPR allocated a half-million dollars for construction and refurnishing. At the end of the summer season a crew of workers began a full winter's work, duplicating the west wing of the original structure on a site just a few feet to the south of the copied wing, giving the hotel the basic north-south orientation it has maintained until today.[2] The two wings were joined by a low split-level wooden passageway.

The hotel's new appearance created a local journalistic furor. A news clipping from 1903 claims that one could march an army of 3,000 men into the building. The reporter envisions soldiers five abreast swinging through the south doors and marching down the main hall, leaving yet enough room for an officer to "pass up and down the line without being crowded to the wall." Considering the commotion caused some years later when a slightly inebriated park warden rode

[2]The west wing of the original building was the main wing of the hotel and the one which Van Horne had meant to front on the river. In fact, because of the blueprint turn-around, it faced Sulphur Mountain and became the west rather than the east wing.

Hotel construction in 1903—essentially duplicating the west wing of the 1888 structure.

The completed 1903 building viewed from Sulphur Mountain.

his horse into the main lobby of the hotel, it's just as well that no one tried to verify the accuracy of the journalist's claim. It's safe to assume, though, that Manager Mathews was well content that his hotel could now house two-thirds again as many as the first hotel's 300 guests. In truth, the closest thing to an army to ever reach the hotel was the celebrated 56th Regiment Iowa National Guard Band of Fort Dodge, Iowa, a great hit at the 1908 summer ball.

As to the interior renovations, it appears that the management continued its previous motif:

It is finished in native wood—Douglas fir—every piece of which has gone through the hands of artistic wood workers. The ceiling and other decorations have been put on in accord with perfect harmony, and the electric lights—well, thousands have been spent on them. The parlours, the sleeping rooms, retreats, refreshment booths, verandahs, baths, and all such are modern and luxurious to the limit.

The 1903 season also witnessed the installation of a complete set of telephones in the hotel, although there had been one phone, one of four in Banff, in the hotel some years earlier. Banff itself was one of the earlier "wired" towns in the west.

But even with a new wing, a new interior, and the luxury of telephones, the hotel could no more accommodate the number of guests desiring rooms in 1903 than it could in 1902. The park superintendent's report sums up the problem:

Some basic roofs:

> No less than 5,000 guests were turned away from Banff during the past season. The Banff Springs Hotel was compelled to remain open for a month later than usual owing to its increasing popularity among the travelling public. Notwithstanding the large additions made to the building in 1903, which includes the addition of over 200 rooms, the management has since found it necessary to make arrangements for yet another large addition. . . .

Gable

As a matter of interest, the proposed addition was to be built "with a view to being utilized throughout the winter." Such a theme was a common one in Banff from 1900 until well into the 1920's, with merchants claiming that each succeeding winter would be *the* winter which would establish Banff as a major winter resort. The Banff Springs Hotel was certainly not immune to the pull of such speculative possibilities, and progressive generations of managers toyed with the idea of making the hotel a year-round resort. Not until 1969 did the hotel become a twelve-month establishment.

Hipped

The exact nature of the "large addition" of 1904, or the addition of 1905, is not known for sure, but it is at least possible that during these years two six-storey frame towers were constructed, one tower apiece for the north and south wings. With their steep-hipped and dormered roofs the towers bore a strong resemblance to the ones which occupy similar positions today.

Hipped-gable

There is evidence to suggest the towers were not constructed until a somewhat later date than 1904 and 1905.[3] If they were indeed constructed in those early years, it is more than likely that one of the first guests to enjoy the elevated view provided by the towers was Joe Cannon, the long-time Speaker of the U.S. House of Representatives. Cannon checked into the hotel during the season of 1905 with a large retinue of fellow legislators and their wives. One wonders what "Uncle Joe," who once vowed that the House would spend "not one cent for scenery," thought of the Canadian Rockies.

In 1906 another small luxury item found its place among the steadily growing "comforts" recorded for the Banff Springs when six arc lights were erected along the high road to the hotel. No reports indicate popular sentiment concerning this particular innovation, although it does appear that most folks were impressed with the technology of the lights and the very act of erecting the lamps, a problem not made easier by six Italians on the crew who spoke no English.

The alterations continued during the winter of 1906-07 when a crew of some 70 men worked almost continuously to build a new boiler, engine and laundry room. The new addition, located at the southeast end of the hotel, was considered unique because it was constructed entirely of river boulders and featured a 90-foot smokestack which, as a news clipping of the day informs us, "it is safe to say will be recorded on many hundreds of photographic films before the season is over."

The only thing that outpaced CPR construction during these years was, again, the number of persons wanting to make use of the construction. There seemed to be no end to the problem. When the hotel opened in May of 1907 it was promptly filled to capacity with 450 registered guests, the start of another overflow season. The trend continued in 1908 and 1909, and during the summer of 1910 the hotel sent close to 400 persons back to the CPR station to find shelter in sleeping cars at $1.50 per night. During that summer

[3]The CPR records show that the towers were not up before the spring of 1911, but long-time residents of Banff maintain that they were built sometime before that year. Where the truth of the matter lies doesn't seem to be too critical at this late date.

The hotel and high road circa 1910. Note the towers on the hotel's wings.

the hotel entertained at least two parties notable enough to make the local paper: a convention of over 100 Winnipeg businessmen; and the Maharaja of Boroda, accompanied by the Maharini, their two children and a large retinue of friends and servants.

And, if the season of 1910 were sublimely busy, the season of 1911 approached the ridiculous. Well over 22,000 persons stayed at the hotel over the course of the summer, and it was noted that "the record of meals served per month at the hotel has exceeded by 2,000 the figure of the great Seattle fair season of two years ago."[4] There were two or three dances a week, the tennis courts were full to overflowing every day that

[4] Seattle fairs have always been good to Banff. Most merchants today remember with fondness the summer season of 1962, the year Seattle hosted a world's fair.

Green fees, 1911:
$ .50 for 18 holes
$1.00 for a day
$5.00 for a week

the weather permitted such sport, and a brand new golf course, built under the direction of a golfing expert brought in from Scotland, saw some 1,500 guests try its greens during the first nine weeks of its existence.

While the folks downtown fulminated about the growing number of "roughs" in town—the "class of visitor who make the Banff trip as an excuse for a glorious drunk," the Banff Springs was spending a bit of time worrying not about quality but about quantity. The quantity of quality remained the greatest problem the hotel faced.

VI

Balconies and Towers, Turrets, Time, and Troubles

*the Châteaux of the Loire . . .
or is it early William Randolph Hearst?*

By 1910 it was apparent that the piecemeal approach to construction which the hotel had pursued for the previous decade could not hope to solve the institution's more pressing problems. Furthermore, the staggering headcount for the 1910 and 1911 seasons, including those persons who had been bedded down at the railway station, emphasized the point that the hotel's potential was falling far short of fulfillment. The well-groomed men of Montreal bent their greying temples together in conference and announced what appeared to be a simple answer: begin work on a new Banff Springs Hotel. And where the old hotel had been the "largest and finest mountain resort on the continent," make the new hotel larger and finer yet.

Whether the planners of 1910 envisioned a completely new structure, one to be built in stages over

Some basic arches:

Circular

Horseshoe

Lancet

Tudor

a number of years, or merely a greatly modified and integrated structure involving the old components, is difficult to determine, but their decision to alter significantly the hotel's appearance and create something "new" was the key element in the evolution of the building which stands today, completed in 1928.

The man commissioned to design the "new" hotel was Walter S. Painter, an American who had been working as the chief architect for the CPR since 1905. Painter was acquainted with Banff and the Banff Springs Hotel at the time of the commission, having visited the community in the years before 1911. Indeed, it seems most likely that he was directly involved with much of the Banff Springs development in the years between 1903 and 1911.

As an architect, Painter was influenced by Price's works and the whole of the CPR château tradition; he was to prove himself an able successor to Price's throne. (Price had died in 1903.) The CPR had begun to stray from the château style by 1910, especially in its designs for city hotels,[1] but the château was still held to be an appropriate mode for all mountain resorts, and Painter was treated to an extensive tour of the Loire region of France before he began to draw up plans for the new Banff Springs.

As a matter of incidental interest, Painter's trip to the Loire poses some intriguing questions for the person interested in the Banff Springs' stylistic origins. Painter spent his summer in the Loire studying and sketching superb examples of the unadulterated French château, and then came home to build a structure which is almost entirely lacking in the features which characterize the French medieval style! The dormers of the present hotel are flat rather than pointed; the arches are circular rather than lancet; the windows of the central tower are round-headed, features which are more indicative of the Scottish baronial tradition than of the pure French château.

[1]One need look no further than the Royal Alexander Hotel in Winnipeg (1904-06) or the Palliser Hotel in Calgary (1911-14) for evidence.

Painter's sketch for a "new" Banff Springs. Only the Centre Tower, however, was completed as sketched—other plans, designed by J. W. Orrock, were used in constructing new wings 13 years after the completion of the tower.

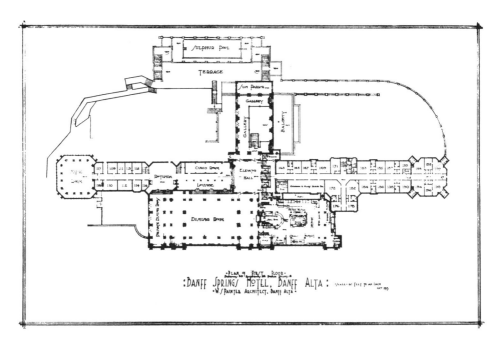

Painter's floor plan, dated October, 1913.

The problem has at least two answers. The Scottish baronial style of the sixteenth and seventeenth centuries was heavily influenced by the Loire châteaux, and Painter was probably interested in seeing the original source material. And the CPR was anxious to exploit the well-nurtured (and largely mythic) conception that the Banff of the Canadian Rockies somehow resembles the fishing village of Banff in Scotland. This latter theme has played an important part in the projected image of Banff and the Banff Springs Hotel since the turn of the century, and it has even been speculated that Price's 1888 structure was designed with a Scottish manse in mind. This though, is doubtful, and, besides, the original building was much too loose a structure to allow such archaeological pinpointing.

At any rate, the hotel, as finished in 1928, is one which owes much archaeologically to both the French and Scottish styles but which, in fact, represents an exacting copy of neither. Nor is it, as one visitor has suggested, "early William Randolph Hearst." It is, as was the original hotel, its own building, diverse in influence and rich in design.

The first step in the creation of the new building was taken shortly after the hotel closed at the end of the 1911 season. A crew of some 200 men started to work at tearing out the existing centre portion of the hotel and preparing foundations for a new reinforced concrete middle wing. The new wing was to become part of an eleven-storey centre tower, given advanced billing as the tallest building in the Canadian Rockies.

But most of the work that first winter went toward the completion of the centre wing and the development of two new swimming pools and a series of bathing rooms. The number of men on the job, many of them brought to town by the CPR, gave Banff its "finest winter to date," and the local paper reported happily that the winter sports club and the hockey club were very active all winter. The influx of men also created the first recorded housing shortage in Banff.

The work on the wing and the pools was completed by the early spring of 1912, and the finished product gave full support to the notion that the new structure was to be a very grand affair. The pools and baths were particularly impressive. A Calgary newspaper reported that the Banff Springs Hotel opened the season with "the finest bathing establishment on the continent," while the Banff paper mentioned a "general air of luxury" about the place.

The "establishment" consisted of three terraces. The outer and lower one was a semi-circular cold, fresh-water pool, while the second terrace held a warm sulphur pool, 28 feet by 80 feet, heated to 110°, and separated from the outer pool by a graceful loggia. The second terrace also contained complete Turkish and Russian baths with no less than 100 individual dressing rooms. The Turkish baths, with their full marble partitions and walls and their floors of imported English tile, proved to be the most popular. They were, sniffed a local journalist, "quite the best part of the Dominion," although the same fellow complained that "it would be more comfortable in the dressing rooms if there were wooden gratings to stand on instead of the bare concrete floors." The third and final terrace consisted of cooling rooms, private sulphur baths, and rooms for an imported Swedish masseur, while the roof to the third terrace functioned as a wide promenade. All things considered, there was indeed a general air of luxury about the baths.

Loggia: an arcaded gallery built into or projecting from the side of a building, particularly one overlooking an open court.

Turkish bath: a bath in which the bather passes through a series of steam rooms of increasing temperatures and then receives a rubdown, massage, and cold shower.

Russian bath: similar to the Turkish bath but without the massage or cold plunge.

One of the first people to enjoy the use of the new baths was none other than the Duke of Connaught. The Duke (the brother of King Edward) and Duchess (the Princess Louise Margaret Alexandra Victoria Agnes of Prussia) stopped briefly at the hotel on their first Canadian transcontinental journey, and the Duke promised to return, saying ". . . my only regret is that I have so short a time to enjoy the many attractions which are presented by Banff and its vicinities."

Although construction was halted for the duration of the 1912 season, by mid-September the various hammerings and bangings associated with heavy structural creation could be heard above the roar of the Bow Falls. A crew even larger than the one used in 1911 was employed for the winter work of 1912, some estimates ranging as high as 600 men, although it is doubtful that there were ever more than 400 involved with the hotel at any one time.

The work for the next two winters was clear cut: build the tallest building in the Canadian Rockies, by hand, before the start of the 1914 season. Walter Painter undertook the contract himself and promised to complete the work in two winter's time, a task most persons considered impossible.

The building process was a slow, arduous, and, by today's standards, dramatic one. Most of the labour was hand labour, and the men had access to none of the ingenious mechanical devices which help modern contractors toss up a 20-storey International-style office building in a few months today. Tons of materials were hauled by wagon from the CPR station to the building site and then pushed and pulled into position by the brute force mustered by the builders.

Elaborate scaffolding, the construction of which seems nearly as awesome as the work on the hotel itself, was first erected and then enclosed in planks to give the men some protection from the frigid winter winds and the snow which seemed at times to rise more quickly than the tower. But the work did progress, and within thirteen months the hotel manager was able to announce that the "alterations" were almost complete. Painter, it appeared, would make his impossible contract.

The completed structure, known as the Painter Tower and including the preliminary work of the centre wing, was 200 feet long, 70 feet wide, and eleven storeys high—a remarkable achievement, given the times and working conditions of the day. It is even more remarkable that during the entire course of construction only two reported architectural mishaps occurred (although there were no doubt more), neither of which could begin to match the blueprints' about-face of the 1888 construction.

The first problem arose when one of the walls (the east wall of the centre tower) fell a bit out of plumb rather early in its rise. The error was not discovered until the building had reached some five or six storeys and then it was too late to start over again. But the awkward angle was not great and the wall was squared up at that point and the building progressed smoothly upward. Today only the most observant guest

Work on the Centre Tower nears completion, 1912.

will notice the slight jog in the wall as it corrects itself and continues its rise.

The other blunder was revealed one afternoon when the building was very near completion. One of the construction foremen called Sam Ward, a joiner on the crew, over to him and, pointing to one of the high dormered windows, asked Sam if he remembered anything about the room behind the window. Sam was unsure and the two of them went to investigate. The mystery began to unravel itself when the two men arrived at the proper spot for an entrance to the room and found nothing but a smooth, finished wall. Sam found a pry bar and, while the foreman winched, drove it between the studs. A room was indeed behind the wall and a crew was called up to put a door into an area which might have been sealed off yet.

Nearly everyone agreed the work on the new tower was superb, but if any one element drew universal acclaim it was the stonework. The CPR, to do things properly, had imported Italian stonecutters and Scottish masons, reputedly the best in the world at their respective jobs, to handle the rock facing on the tower.

The facing consists of Mount Rundle limestone, taken from a quarry a little over a half-mile distant from the hotel. Once quarried, the rock was hauled by wagon to the building site where the masons would do the final shaping and laying of the blocks. This particular job proved to be most tedious, as the sedimentary rock is brittle and tends to split and break easily. But the cutters and masons proved equal to their reputations and, as an observant guest might notice today, the rock work of the centre tower is really very good—far better than the work done in later years on the two wings. The earlier work is of a consistency and quality which in probability couldn't be duplicated today—even if an organization willing to underwrite the expense of an attempt could be found.

The rock work held a surprise for the people working on the hotel. It changed colour! The rock, as quarried, has a bluish-grey tinge to it which changes to a rich brown colour with extended exposure to the sun, and with some incredulity early labourers returned to the hotel after a few years' absence to discover their blue castle turned to brown. Today's guest can observe the difference between the two shades of rock by finding an area of the building protected from direct sunlight and matching the rock found there to the general tone of the whole building.

One other architectural aspect of the centre tower leads to speculation—the great chunk of bedrock —which forms an integral part of the northern wall of the tower (visible where the tower joins the north wing on the river side of the hotel). It was, of course, an architectural decision to incorporate the bedrock into the wall, probably to save the effort of knocking out a particularly resistant piece of rock and to add a fine ornamental touch to the structure. The presence of the rock could certainly be used as a facetious argument against any who might claim that Painter's architecture lacked an "organic" sense. Actually, there is one other piece of bedrock, this piece considerably larger—20 feet by 150 feet—which was never excavated from the hotel's sub-basement. It was simply walled off and, one would suppose, functions as a rather sturdy support for the floors above it.

The Painter Tower was ready for business when the hotel opened in May of 1914. Over two million dollars had been spent on the tower and the new interior, now emphasizing much wicker furniture. The interior was the work of a Mrs. Hayter Reed, a woman of great talent and energy who was responsible for many of the CPR hotels' interiors from the early 1900's to the 1920's. She was responsible for the various Banff Springs interiors from 1905, when she and her husband[2] lived in Banff, to the late 1920's when the present interior was designed by Michael Delahanty and Kate Treleaven.

Mrs. Hayter Reed: a woman of great energy, responsible for many of the early CPR Hotel interiors.

[2]Mr. Reed was a frontiersman of sorts who was instrumental in the signing of the Indian Treaty No. 7 in 1877. After the treaty was signed, Reed was hired to work for the CPR. He became involved with management of the CP hotels and eventually became General Superintendent of Hotels, CPR.

The hotel with the completed centre (Painter) tower. (Compare with the older hotel, page 40.)

The new tower included a dining room, a large rotunda which became the central lobby for the hotel, and bedrooms for over 300 guests. Much of the new public floor space was done in red English tile, still very much in evidence, a feature which has led to the despair of many a bellboy in the intervening years, as the bellboys are responsible for keeping each individual tile outlined with a fresh coat of black paint. The meticulous construction of the building as a whole was not going to be diminished by inattention to the smallest detail of upkeep.

VII

A Parade of Princes,
Politicians and Patrons

"as happy as grigs
whatever a grig may be"

Although Painter's sketches had provided for
two new wings as well as a new tower for the Banff
Springs—meaning, in effect, a completely new structure
—his part in the construction came to an end with the
completion of the centre tower. Upon completion of
the tower the upper echelons of the CPR decided to
sit back a bit and see how things ran with the new
tower and the two older wings.[1] It was to be fourteen
years before the rest of Painter's plans, with major
modifications by another architect, was to become a
reality of steel, concrete, and rock.

The intervening years were prosperous for the
hotel, and successive managements worked diligently to
maintain and improve the hotel's established reputation

[1]Actually, "sitting back" for the CPR in those days
merely meant slowing down to half-throttle, for the
company was still under the influence of Van
Horne's dictum that anytime the company was not
dynamically expanding it was moving backwards,
degenerating. There was no middle ground.

as one of the great luxury resorts on the continent. Over the years the hotel had become more and more of a summer home for a number of the guests, and by 1914 many of the people staying at the hotel were seasoned Banff veterans with ten or twelve years of "Springing" to their credit.

The Duke and Duchess of Connaught became seasonal repeats when they returned in August of 1914 for a two-week stay, their retinue occupying 22 rooms of the new tower, with an additional ten rooms for servants' quarters. But if the Duke had regrets about leaving Banff in 1912, he had even greater regrets about departing in 1914.

Coming back into Banff after a canoe trip down the Bow River one afternoon, the Duke saw a line of scarlet-clad Mounties standing in rank at the North Landing. His guide, Jim Brewster, heard him say, to no one in particular, "Ah, yes, I expected this." Then he lapsed into a profound silence until they reached the landing and beached the canoe. The Mounties presented him with Great Britain's Declaration of War and instructed him a train was waiting at the station. Within a few hours the Duke found himself steaming east across the prairies, heading toward home and the Great War.

In the following year another guest had regrets about leaving Banff, but for other reasons. Carrying a light fishing rod and speaking vociferously, the Roughrider President of the United States, Teddy Roosevelt, was in town and staying at the Springs. Banff, it appears, appealed to him:

> I am DEE-LIGHTED with your town. Banff is the centre of all that is beautiful, and this part of the mountains is the Yellowstone Park of Canada. I regret exceedingly my time is so limited as nothing would give me greater pleasure than to spend several weeks catching your justly celebrated mountain trout.

The parade of princes, politicians, and patrons continued unhampered throughout the decade, and in 1920 the hotel expanded its celebrity horizons by entertaining the Hollywood cast of *Conceit*, starring

such greats as Betty Hilburn, Maurice Costello, Hedda
Hopper, and William Davidson. It was the first of
many movies to be filmed near Banff, and the word
spread quickly concerning the Canadian Rockies. Glam-
ourous names associated with the film world began to
appear more frequently on the pages of the Banff
Springs Register.

The hotel, in the meantime, if not expanding,
was keeping itself busy with renovation and innovation.
The east wing of the 1888 building, which had served
for many years as the dining room and kitchen for the
original structure, was torn down in 1915, and some
400 guest rooms were redecorated for the start of the
1916 season.

The summer of 1916 also introduced Japanese
bellboys and waitresses. A lady journalist was hired to
act as a society press agent, her job to chronicle "the
arrival and doings of all prominent society people" and
to see that such arrivals and doings were distributed to
the press throughout North America.

Other alterations occurred during the winter
of 1916 when the hotel was allotted $140,000 for the
construction of another new boiler house and laundry;

and in 1917 the hotel turned the management of the golf course over to the government with the understanding the course would be expanded to 18 holes. Apparently the only thing not altered in some fashion was the telephone service, for one visitor remarked that one had as much chance of reaching the desired party "as winning the pot against a royal flush."

Actually, one other complaint was levied against the hotel during the 1914-1920 period, but it did not originate with the guests. The CPR, by virtue of possessing a railroad which ran through Banff, a railway station at Banff, and a large hotel in Banff, exercised a healthy power of persuasion over the potential visitors to Banff. Simply by advertising the CPR hotels on CPR trains and making sure the CPR tallyho held the favoured platform position at the CPR station, the company ensured a capacity level crowd for the Banff Springs Hotel.

The other hotels in town developed resentments toward such lopsided arrangements, and in the summer of 1915 several of the managers arranged a meeting with two CPR officials to air the problem. The company listened to the charges and promised to alter the position of the hack stands (although the Banff Springs would maintain its number one spot) and arrange for literature concerning accommodation in Banff to be circulated on the trains. Otherwise, they remained adamant the CPR hotel would retain all other "privileges of the platform."

The settlement temporarily soothed most tempers, but in August the local newspaper ran an editorial which, while stating it had no particular desire to roast the CPR, presented evidence that someone connected with the CPR in the east was advising railway passengers the Banff Springs Hotel was the only hotel in Banff, and that if travellers couldn't get a reservation at the Springs they'd be wise to travel on without stopping.

That such advice was dispersed seems without a doubt true. After all, it was "vouched for by residents of unimpeachable integrity." But whether such advice was dispersed maliciously or merely through mis-information seems an open question. Another editorial in

the same August paper provides an interesting if perhaps unwitting insight into the attack on the hotel.
The 1915 season was supposed to be a banner year for
Banff, but it fell far short of anticipations. The editorial suggests the CPR's "dog-in-the-manger" attitude
was responsible for the situation. The article claims
that lack of CPR (and government) advertising about
the Rocky Mountain Park and the possibilities of good
accommodation in Banff lost much business from tourists returning to the east from the Pacific Exposition.
It was thought that these people were choosing southern routes through other, better advertised areas such
as the Grand Canyon. The whole problem, when
viewed with the smug advantage of hindsight, appears
to have centred about the search for a scapegoat for a
less than terrific season.[2]

[2]The Great War would also have been a considerable
factor in reducing the flow of tourists to Banff.

A four-horse stage loads for sight-seeing, 1920's.

The argument was never clearly resolved. The winter interlude of 1915-16 seems to have cooled whatever heat had been generated, for the problems of platform privileges and mis-representation were never mentioned again.

An early Mrs. Reed interior at the Banff Springs.

Life at the hotel swept on unaffected. The Duke of Connaught finally managed a full two weeks at the hotel during the summer of 1916, and, outside of the occasional (and ultimately, in any large hotel, expected) bizarre occurrence, such as the non-fatal shooting of a man in 1920[3] and an equally intriguing charge of "bigamy" levied against two staff members in 1922, the palace prepared itself for a decade of gracious living. So gracious, indeed, that when an old-timer named Morley Roberts, who had helped put the railroad through Banff in 1883, returned in 1925 he found the hotel somewhat beyond credulity:

> The truth is that I could not take beautiful Banff seriously. I dreamed it, and like so many dreams it was at once absurd and beautiful. On a pine-covered bank or bluff above the crystal foam of the Bow I came to a gigantic castle. It had no business being there, for when I was thereabouts so long ago no one could have thought of it. It was full of most curious looking people who seemed very busy about nothing at all but were as happy as grigs, whatever a grig may be. They wore all kinds of odd costumes. Some women, so greatly determined on being noticed as to defy ridicule flaunted about in long shining boots and scarlet jackets and jockey caps, while others wore clothes "made in America" in the back woods, which looked as if they had been cut out with an axe. The dream-castle was full of such people who talked all at once and I saw in a moment that they were not real. I, or someone else, had imagined them. If any of us workers of the old days had seen their likes we should have thought we had delirium tremens at the least.

A CPR pamphlet from the 1920's. Good advice for the first-time visitor to the Rockies.

For the guests of the hotel, however, there was no question of reality—life was as socially painful (or ecstatic) as it had ever been. Just as the towns-people conducted their periodic raids on old Jim Toy's Laundry, looking for Chinese Whiskey and opium, so the British guests conducted their periodic raids on the ever-suffering American guests. According to the local paper dated August 12, 1922:

> A newly rich American, a class which is flooding the country just now, approached an English

[3]Local reportage of the day gives no insight into the why or how of the incident, only the where and when.

A CPR tallyho swings up Banff Avenue on its way to the hotel.

gentleman in the Banff Springs Hotel recently with the query: 'Say, where is the lavatory?' The Englishman coolly looked his questioner over and replied: 'Go down that corridor and turn to the right where you will see a door with the sign "Gentlemen" on it, but don't let that deter you, old top.'

As regular as clockwork, the cycles moved inexorably on through the years.

VIII

Out of the Fire
Its Wings are Stretched

"The level chambers, ready with their pride,
were glowing to receive a thousand guests."
— JOHN KEATS

By 1925 the time had arrived for the completion of the plans begun in 1911. As early as the fall of 1921 the CPR authorized nearly two million dollars for the destruction of the old wooden wings of the hotel and their replacement by rock-faced, fireproof structures. And the record season of 1922, which saw 400-500 guests registered daily throughout July and August (a grand seasonal tally of some 52,000 visitors), provided a compelling rationale for further expansion.

The new wings would be built over the course of two years—one to be erected during the winter of 1926-27, and the other to follow suit during the winter of 1927-28. First it was necessary for a separate annex to be built, a structure which would serve as substitute housing for the regular hotel guests while the wings were being replaced.

A photo taken during the early stages of the 1926 North Wing fire.

Accordingly, at the close of the 1925 season, a 100-room building was erected to the south of and below the hotel's south wing, a structure which, in its grey, cement-finished exterior surface and its decorative allusions to the Tudor style, broke with the rest of the hotel's château motif. The annex today serves as a staff quarters and stands as a rather curious Tudor anomaly amidst the other rock-faced Gothic structures which compose the entirety of the hotel.

The work on the annex was completed toward the end of March, 1926, a date which proved to be none too soon. On the sixth of April, 1926, at 11:00 a.m., the hotel's assistant manager, J. B. Coysh, and a CPR publicity man, Chief B. C. Long Lance, noticed great amounts of smoke curling skyward from the north wing of the hotel. Coysh filed a fire report immediately and within an hour over 500 men were at the hotel, fighting a very businesslike blaze. The old wooden wing burned brightly and rapidly, and by 2:00 p.m. the last of the original 1888 hotel was a smouldering pile of debris. The fire-fighters, including some men who raced in from Calgary, far from being able to save the wing, had to be content with rescuing as much furniture as possible and trying to keep the damage to the fireproof centre tower at a minimum.

The structure of the centre tower, shielding the south wing from harm, sustained grievous injury itself when a major explosion in the basement blew out many of the windows and fittings of the tower. And flames crept inside the centre wing to gut the gracious 13-year-old dining room. Flames from the fire struck both the north and west faces of the centre tower, and the smoke-stained surfaces of the tower can be seen today where the new north wing joins the tower on the river side of the hotel.

The fire itself was attributed to labourers involved in pre-season blasting operations around the base of the north wing, preliminary work for the replacement construction which was to begin at the close of the 1926 season. The workers had built a fire close to the old wing and the flames spread unnoticed to the main building itself.

Rumours at the time suggested a theory that the fire had been set intentionally by workmen under orders from CPR officials (men who knew the wing was to be torn down in the fall anyway), but there is little if any evidence to support that idea. Any such fire would be sure to delay the opening of the hotel, as well as reduce greatly the capacity of the hotel during what promised to be a highly lucrative summer; and the idea that a hotel, any hotel, would risk the adverse publicity of a hotel fire (perhaps the greatest anathema of any hotel owner) is not very solid thinking.

If there were to be a fire, though, it could hardly have happened more fortuitously; unless, of course, it could have happened in the fall of 1926: the wing was to be torn down at the end of the season, plans and moneys existed for a replacement wing, and the fire occurred well before the start of the tourist season—before any guest had arrived who might have been tragically caught in a midsummer blaze.

Following the fire the CPR acted with a speed and precision that would have befitted old Van Horne himself. Sir Edward Beatty, now president of the CPR, was on the scene within a matter of days, and it was decided that construction on the new wing would begin immediately. A generous budget of two million dollars was allocated for the construction of the

The North Wing, the last of the original building, lies a smouldering ruins. Extensive Centre Tower damage visible.

wing and the work necessary for the restoration of the centre tower. Work was well underway when the hotel belatedly opened its doors on July 1, 1926.

The man in charge of designing the new wings was J. W. Orrock, whose ideas were compatible with Painter's. Using the general style of the old wooden wings (to which Painter also paid homage in his 1911 sketches for a new hotel), Orrock penned the final additions to the hotel which stands today, making both the north and south wings much larger than those Painter had drawn, angling the towers of the wings gracefully away from the river. He enlarged the centre tower and modified its roofline, thus tying the earlier structure solidly to the new wings.

The north wing, of course, was the first to be replaced, and the work proceeded rapidly, although not so smoothly as one might wish. In October one man was killed and two others seriously injured when a lift

68

derrick collapsed and a steel beam weighing some 2,500 pounds dropped a full three storeys onto the men working below. In February another accident saw a man badly injured as he looked down an elevator shaft, yelling at a man on the lower floor to send up some tile. His powers of timing or observation, or both, were a bit off and the lift came down on his head from above. Construction humour allowed that Bill lost his head in the excitement of getting the tile laid. In truth, his head remained connected to his body and he survived to work another day. The elevator though, was not to be robbed of its grisly prize, and in May it claimed the life of a man who was trying to grease it, an accident held to be the unfortunate fellow's own fault.

Destruction of the old South Wing, 1926. It is interesting to note the horse and wagon technology at work.

The actual structural work of the north wing followed closely the same general procedure as that which went into the centre tower fourteen years earlier: a steel frame was erected, and then, around the steel, a massive plank cocoon, a shelter for the workmen who continued with the concrete and rock work throughout the winter. In the spring of 1927, less than a year after the great fire, the cocoon fell away and a new blue limestone wing stretched toward the distant peak of Cascade Mountain.

The work on the north wing was considered typical of CPR construction jobs, exhibiting speed and efficiency in completing a given task, but the work on the south wing was even faster. The old wing was torn down at the close of the 1926 season, but construction on the new wing did not begin until the end of the 1927 season, in September. Seven months later, in April, 1928, the southern wing emerged from its plank cocoon. If this feat were not phenomenal in itself, the crew also found time to extend and rebuild the inner and outer swimming pools, enclosing the inner pool (thus necessitating a switch to non-sulphured waters

Steel framing for the South Wing, 1927. Note the extensive additions which were made to the Painter Tower by Orrock's construction of the North Wing. (Comparative photo, page 53.)

Construction progress on the South Wing: steel framing, protective plank cocoon erected and removed, and the finished product. The first photo is dated August 8, 1927; the last, March 30, 1928.

for the inner pool to avoid gassing the entire hotel), and to erect the hotel's upper annex, the staff quarters which stand directly south of the south wing.

The swift pace with which the work proceeded (again, as in the 1911-14 period, largely without mechanical aid) insured the hotel would be in readiness for the start of the 1928 season. As spring yielded to summer, people throughout North America and Europe learned that for the second time in 15 years a "new" Banff Springs Hotel was awaiting their arrival. An inspection team from the CPR, headed by none other than Sir Edward himself, was on hand for the opening ceremonies of the 1928 Banff Springs, the hotel which stands today.

Incidentally, Beatty and his crew were none too early for their inspection tour that spring, for it seems that whenever he turned his back, a carpenter or mason would appear from some dark corner to put a quick finishing touch on some not quite completed portion of the hotel. Such activities were discreetly undertaken and kept as distant as possible from Sir Edward, as he had been promised the hotel would be "finished" upon his arrival. Much to the credit of the workmen, Beatty never did learn of their secretive hammerings and polishings.

Nor did he ever learn of a sealed-off room which still stands dark and empty somewhere at the junction of the north wing and the centre tower. The man who sealed off the room can no longer exactly remember where it is and, unlike the sealed room in the centre tower, this one has no window to offer any clue of its mute existence.

But if Beatty would have been surprised to learn of a "dead" room in the hotel, he would have been even more surprised to learn his company had financed the construction of two private residences in Banff. It seems that one of the men lorrying supplies from the CPR station to the hotel during the 1927-28 period had a chronic problem keeping a full load on his wagon. Part of each shipment fell off at a particular spot along the route and he never managed to get it all back on. That the lost materials miraculously arose from the dust *en route* to form two pleasant houses was another secret Beatty never learned.

Beatty did learn, however, that highly polished oak floors can be slippery and, recovering his balance and his dignity after a near tumble in the Alhambra Dining Room (which had originally been planned as a ballroom), he ordered the entire floor, so painstakingly and expensively finished, be carpeted immediately.

On the whole, though, Beatty found the hotel much to his liking. If the original hotel had been a place of elegance and refinement, the new hotel was one of haughty grandeur. It was, in short, one of the most beautifully and carefully finished buildings on the continent, and no expense had been spared to make it so.

The external appearance of the hotel, despite different building periods and architects, presents a homogenous appearance. Its style is ultimately its own, although the Scottish (and thus, implicity, French) influence is not to be denied. And the hotel still exhibits those features which Bruce Price considered essential for a northern building: massive wall surfaces and steep roofs.

The interior elements of the hotel, on the other hand, are as mis-matched as the exterior elements are matched. Still, the various styles discovered within the building complement each other and even add a richness to the hotel's atmosphere which might be lacking were the interior consistent throughout. Furthermore, the disparate elements reflect, to a certain extent, the nature of the great European castles where succeeding scions would alter portions of the manse to fit their own tastes and the changing styles of the times.

Overall, the various styles encountered in the hotel, ranging across the breadth of Gothic and Renaissance architecture and decoration, and exhibiting influences of England, France, Scotland, Switzerland and Spain, combine to keep alive the suggestion of an elegant and romantic past.[1] In this regard the hotel fulfills the ideal of all the early CPR hotels as propounded by Van Horne and Price.

But perhaps even more fascinating than the different styles encountered within the various rooms of the hotel is the lavish and detailed presentation of the styles. In keeping with Banff Springs tradition, the CPR spared no expense in the decoration of the hotel.

[1]For a more detailed description of the periods represented in the suites, public spaces, and furniture pieces of the hotel, see the Appendix at the back of the book.

In order to enhance the Spanish motif of the Alhambra Dining Room the company had the great bronze doors which now grace its entrance wrought at a cost of $30,000. For the eight arched windows which provide the "million dollar view" from the Riverview Lounge, the company brought glass across the continent in a custom-fitted box car.[2] Bedford lime flagstones were shipped in for the floor of Mount Stephen Hall, and for certain stairways, fireplaces, and windowsills the company imported the famous fossiliferous Tyndall stone from Garson, Manitoba.

The Tyndall stone constitutes a particularly unusual feature of the hotel. The stone is heavily fossilized and very soft, which makes it an easy material to work·with. It has been used to good effect in decorative work in many public buildings in Canada, and the CPR was quick to realize its potential for the Banff Springs. In places where the rock has been worn, such as on the circular stairway near the Alhambra Dining Room, it takes on a special lustre and the fossils stand out in high relief. The overall effect is most intriguing. As one guest discovered while listening to a concert in Mount Stephen Hall one evening:, "A strange emotion comes over one who traces with his finger a fossilized trilobite on a window-sill while listening to the music of a modern orchestra."

The company, of course, was determined to have workmanship commensurate with the quality of the imported materials, and officials demanded that the greatest care be exhibited in the execution of the most minute decorative detail. The oaken wainscoting, the linenfold work, the animal carvings, the delicate plasterwork of the ceilings (an especially beautiful example is the mushroom ceiling of the circular stairway near the Alhambra), the highly polished terrazzo floors, the stained glass work, the great carved oak beams of Mount Stephen Hall, and the numerous and varied

Wainscoting: a wood lining or panelling on the walls of a room.

Linenfold: wood or stone carved to depict folded linen.

Terrazzo: a floor material of broken stones and cement polished in place.

[2]The workmen who were responsible for installing the great windows were horrified one afternoon to find their foreman staggering across the stacked glass, hiccuping and waving an empty bottle in the air. It turned out it was an act for the men: the boss knew the glass's strength when horizontal and stacked, and he also knew that his men didn't.

gargoyles which peer at unsuspecting guests from dark corners—all exhibit a patience and devotion to fine craftsmanship which has all but disappeared in the recent era of plastic imitation, prefabrication, and automation. As one staff member takes pride in pointing out, even the radiator covers are minor masterpieces.

The furnishing of the "new" hotel, a feature of the Banff Springs which today draws as much comment as the general architecture of the building, is a major factor in creating the rich, textured baronial atmosphere of the hotel. The tapestries, prints, rugs, and furniture pieces were selected by Michael Delahanty, a former manager of the hotel, and Kate Treleaven, a personal secretary to Sir Edward Beatty. The Leonardo Society of Montreal also helped with the reproduction selection.

The elements comprising the present interior were chosen coterminously with the 1927-28 construction and the new decor was presented in its entirety for the first time with the hotel's opening in 1928. Aside from a few pieces of wicker furniture found in the conservatory, the early interiors of Mrs. Reed disappeared with the last of the old wings.

The furniture itself, representing an even greater variety of styles and periods than the interior architecture, was made by the Montreal firm of Castle & Son Manufacturing, and all pieces are exact reproductions of original period furniture. The reproduction work is, in fact, so precise that the plane marks on the original surfaces are exhibited in the reproductions. The pieces chosen for reproduction were found in various European castles and manors, many of the articles reputedly coming from castles and manses near Banff in Scotland.

Many of the prints which grace the walls of the hotel are Gothic and Renaissance in origin and are certainly in keeping with the general milieu of the great halls. It is interesting to note, though, that during the thirties some of the prints in private rooms were often discovered turned face-to-the-wall or were taken down completely—they were simply too sombre for some of the guests. One particularly interesting wall decoration is the large multi-coloured tapestry found in the reception hall. It was made from pieces of soldiers' uniforms by a nurse who worked on the battlefields of the Crimean War.

The hotel prides itself on its wide selection of furniture pieces, oriental rugs, and excellent prints, and it maintains a large workshop with a full-time staff to keep the pieces in good repair. At one time the hotel kept a "furniture blueprint" of all the public spaces in the building—plans which showed exactly where each piece of furniture, mirror, print and rug was to be placed and kept.

All in all, the hotel, as opened in 1928, exhibited quite a profusion of disparate styles and objects, large and small, which, by virtue of their good taste and excellent craftsmanship, managed to fall together to create a great and feudal atmosphere—a scene set beautifully for the most exciting era the hotel was ever to know.

Banff

Through enchanted portals Banff welcomes you into a great baronial hall where light streams down over shining armour and buffalo heads and the happy-hearted, do-as-we-please life that is Banff. Gay groups in riding and golfing outfits. Trail riders and hikers making a jolly fuss about getting off. Happy tourists bustling in and out of busses. Wide-eyed children in blanket coats and sombreros. Smiling Jap bell boys darting about with luggage.

IX

Of a Brief
But Golden Moment

"Who are they,
these butterfly ladies in their Paris gowns?"

In the long and glittering history of the Banff
Springs Hotel, one era is particularly dazzling, that
span of time stretching from the completion of the
"new" hotel to the outbreak of World War Two. During this period of the late 1920's and 30's the hotel
seemed to achieve a perfect blend of the realities of
day-to-day hotel life and all the preconceived fantasies
one might hold of life at a luxury hotel: the reality
and the myth fused and became one and the same.

Not that anything much had changed from
the earlier days, at least on a superficial level: princes
and politicians still frequented the halls, money flowed
easily through familiar hands, the traditions of the
hotel remained the same (even though the physical
plant of the building had been altered), and comments
made concerning the hotel carried the same tenor in
1937 as in 1897. Indeed, just as a prominent New York
journalist could claim in 1909 that:

Between New York and Shanghai . . . there is
no spot more cosmopolitan than the rotunda of
the C.P. Hotel at Banff. . . . The women in this
group of people in the rotunda of the hotel are
dressed as attractively as any women in any hotel
in the world, and when the orchestra plays and
the people move about talking to each other I
could imagine myself in Buenos Aires, in Bom-
bay, in Melbourne, in Malta, in Cape Town or
in any other city in which the currents of the
world come together.

so could a London writer exclaim in 1937:

Of one or two places in the world it has been
said that if we would but bide there a while we
would see all our friends, in due course, pass by.
Of such and such a chair at the Café de la Paix
in Paris that has been said, and of the Strand
Corner, in London, by Charing Cross. To the
number of these places I would add the Banff
Springs Hotel. Sit in the portico there, and in
due time all your old friendships will be re-
newed.

But there was, somehow, a difference between
that earlier pre-Great War era, characterized by the
brisk and measured step of propriety, and the *entre
deux guerres* era, perhaps best characterized by the
phrase "cultured ease," which found its fullest expres-
sion in the 1930's.

The change in general attitude registered at
the hotel, though, was a reflection of changes in the
world at large. The Great War dealt a crushing blow
to the moneyed classes of Europe, who, in High Victorian idealism, considered themselves responsible for,
and in control of, the ebb and flow of the world's
fortunes. Such an image of importance pointed toward
a logical social conclusion of great emphasis on personal propriety—one had to wear the responsibilities of
one's money in an exemplary fashion.

The war was not a pretty one; and the self-
congratulatory esteem of the wealthy classes disappeared in the dark smoke hanging over the Marne,
Vimy Ridge, and Ypres. At the armistice little was left

One of the old White buses prepares to leave on a sightseeing trip about 1934.

of the previous social tradition, and a new and significantly broader-based social stratification emerged from the crumbled and shattered ways of life.

More important than the breakdown of the social structure was the breakdown of the concepts which accompanied it. The rich and socially ranked people of the world (from which the Banff Springs drew much of its clientèle) began to view themselves and their money in a new light, and they began to effect an escape from what had been thought the responsibilities implicit in wealth. The whale-boned Gibson Girl gave way to the casual flapper of the twenties and the vamp of the thirties. The collar was being loosened.

In time, the depression played its role. For many people the uncertainty of the future forced them into contact with the present for the first time, and their conclusion was that they had better live as fully as possible today.

If the Banff Springs, in its broadest institutional interpretation (including its general milieu as well as its physical structure), had been a "sumptuous affair" at the turn of the century, it was, by 1930, just a bit more than "sumptuous," and where it had been "daring" in previous years, it now became "truly extravagant."

It was against this general setting that many of the most interesting, most amusing, and most warmly human events in the hotel's history occurred. The hotel vibrated with the quirks and idiosyncracies which only great wealth can afford, of those social amenities which come only through a coin-clanking upbringing. It was a time of elegant dress, elegant entertainment, and elegant relationships.

It was a time when people would arrive at the hotel with letters of credit worth $50,000, a sum ear-marked specifically for a 60 to 90 day stay in Banff. "The men," reports an old banker, "would fish and play golf, and the women would change their clothes." There was a staff of ten porters who did nothing but carry luggage from the station to the hotel and back again, and the hotel had to install a special elevator to handle the huge steamer trunks which arrived like herds of buffalo.

It was also a time when the façade of highbrow snobbishness was stretched dangerously thin across a bubbling cauldron of exuberance. Many of the old-time seasonals undoubtedly preferred the more stolid propriety of the pre-war era and certainly lived their lives to that end, but it must have been hard for them to ignore the shrieks of the young New York debutante who, having declared her boredom with life at the hotel, found herself airborne in the direction of the swimming pool, $300 gown and all.

It's also probable that Murray Adaskin, violinist for the Toronto Trio (and later one of Canada's foremost composers) gained a certain "highbrow" perspective the first night the Trio performed at the hotel. The task of the evening was to play for the dinner hour first, and then to give an hour's concert in the Mount Stephen Hall. As the dinner hour approached Murray was notified the Trio was not to play in the dining room itself, but in the foyer to the dining room, and that the volume of the music was to be more *piano* than *forte*. Although a bit taken aback by such curious instructions, the Trio accepted their fate and played gracefully and well throughout the dinner hour. It was not until the hotel manager and his wife emerged from the dining room that the musicians began to understand the motivations behind the directives given them. Approaching the young violinist, the manager smiled and then whispered in his ear: "Just fine, Murray—didn't bother a soul!"

But if the manager weren't able to appreciate fully the Trio's music for what it was, there were many who could. The Mount Stephen concerts, presented

The Toronto Trio. Murray Adaskin, violin; Louis Crerar, piano; and Cornelius Ysselstyn, cello. The trio played eleven seasons at the hotel from 1930 to 1941. Between sets Mr. Crerar composed crossword puzzles, an activity which has probably earned him as much fame as his piano.

six nights a week (on the seventh night a local natur-
alist and author, Dan McCowan, presented a nature
talk), were always very well-received by a discrimi-
nating and knowledgeable audience. Many of the members of the New York and Boston fine arts élite would
spend their summers at the hotel, and for more than
one season Adaskin had his programmes examined and
edited daily by a Mrs. Hall, a prominent patron of the
Boston Symphony.

The arts did, in fact, play a vital role in
creating and maintaining the hotel's image. Under the
auspices of John Murray Gibbon, a CPR promotion
man whose energies and interests seem to have approached the span of those of William Van Horne, the
Light Opera Company of Alfred Heather presented
two operas a week throughout the seasons of 1930-32.
Staged in the ballroom, the operas featured many of
the well-known singers of the day—Randolph Crowes,
Enid Gray, Frances James, and Allan Burt.

Gibbon also introduced a scheme whereby the
top artists and painters of the day—such men as Carl
Rungius and W. J. Phillips—were asked to visit the
hotel and paint the "Canadian Pacific Rockies."[1] The
plan worked well, providing both the hotel and the
artists with excellent publicity, although there is one
memorable occasion when things got a little out of
hand. One day in 1931, Carl Rungius curtly dismissed
from his presence a young man whom he took to be
one of the Japanese bellboys. Carl was making final
preparations for a show of four local artists, Rungius,
Charlie Beil, Nick Grandmaison, and Peter Whyte,
which was to open that afternoon. He was simply not
about to be distracted from his work by any requests
from hotel staff. Only later did Rungius learn the man
had been an emissary from the Queen of Siam, then
visiting the hotel, who wanted to ask for a special
showing for the Queen. The Queen never did visit the
show.

[1]Gibbon would give the artists a return pass to Banff
on the railway in exchange for a painting or paint-
ings which he would reproduce in his colour bro-
chures ·of the Canadian Rockies.

But the emphasis on the arts was merely a sidelight, a rich embellishment, to what the hotel had always been: a top rate mountain resort. Pack trips were more popular than ever, a combination of CPR and government money was developing new trails throughout the mountain parks, and the CPR, by 1930, had developed a number of back-country cabins for people to use as overnight shelters on extended trips into the mountains. Gibbon, partly for personal reasons, partly for Canadian Pacific promotion, established the Trail Riders of the Canadian Rockies, the Skyline Hikers of the Canadian Rockies, and the Ski Runners of the Canadian Rockies, organizations designed to encourage folks to spend more time in the mountains.

Climbing, fishing and canoeing remained popular activities, and golf and tennis were still played by the slope of Mount Rundle.

Two other activities associated with the hotel reached special prominence during the "golden era." One was the Banff Indian Days, an institution already some 40 years old by 1930, and the other was the Banff Highland Gathering and Scottish Music Festival, a comparatively young but very popular Scottish celebration.

By the 1930's the Indian Days had evolved from the smallish gatherings of the 1890's to a somewhat grander celebration in the best tradition of the old West. The activities would begin with the mustering of a great number of Indians at the Indian Grounds some distance north of the townsite. From the Indian

Throwing the diamond hitch.

Grounds the horde would parade into town and up Banff Avenue to the courtyard of the hotel. The colourful parade marked the beginning of several days of singing, dancing and Indian athletic competitions. It was an annual event enjoyed both by the Indian participants and the white observers and served as a good safety-valve for the pressures of a resort-town summer.

Another special Indian Days occasion was witnessed a few years later when Helen Keller visited the Banff Springs during the course of the midsummer festival. The Stonys paid special tribute to the great lady by making her an honorary princess of their tribe.

The other summer festival, usually held in mid-August, was the Highland Gathering. Initiated by the CPR in 1927, the Gathering became somewhat of an annual national event before it faded away in the mid-thirties. The programme notes for the 1931 Gathering provide a little of the flavour of the occasion:

> . . . when the Highland Gathering [came] to Banff, the Scots of Western Canada rolled up in their thousands to attend and take part, the pipes skirled, the dancers danced, and kilts swung and there was a brave array of tartans in the forest clearing under the serrated peaks of these grim, gray Rockies.

The Reverend Charles Gordon, better known as Ralph Connor, preaches a Highland sermon in the Devil's Cauldron.

There was a wide variety of competitions: dancing, including the Highland Fling, the Seann Triubhas, the Sword Dance, the Scottish Reel, and the Sailor's Hornpipe; regimental piping; highland dress; and Caledonian athletics, including racing, hurdles, the hop, step, and jump, the discus, the javelin, pole vaulting, the 16-pound hammer, the 16-pound shot, the 56-pound weight, and tossing the caber. Most of the events took place on the green below the hotel, near the tennis courts, and all were well-attended.

The Highland Gathering was unable to sustain itself for more than a decade, though most of the old guests and townspeople remember it with a special fondness.[2]

[2]The demise of the Gathering has been attributed to the frugal nature of the Scots, who, while enjoying the festivities at the Banff Springs, preferred to save their pennies by taking lodging at the downtown hotels.

The Indian Days and the Highland Gathering were events of a different nature, but they did hold one thing in common: CPR promotion and money.[3] The late '20's and '30's represented an era when the hotel's propensity for extravagance was equal to that of the most extravagant guests. The golf course, for example, once again under CPR management, was considered one of the toughest courses on the continent and featured a special imported southern grass (which proved so popular with the local elk that for many years the course had to be fenced in and locked up at night). And in 1941, when the hotel management decided that the bridle-trail near the building was a bit too dusty, 400 tons of oak tanbark were imported from Ontario to provide a ten-foot wide, four-and-a-half mile long trail which was promptly dubbed "Rotten Row" in honour of London's famous equestrian grounds.

Nor did the "special touches" end with silent, dustless bridle-trails. In the late thirties Benny Goodman wrote to say he'd like to visit the hotel, but could do so only if there were a place to land his plane. The CPR arranged to have a landing strip cleared near the Buffalo Paddock. Goodman did fly in and most of the

[3]Actually, the financial backing for Indian Days became more and more a town responsibility as the years passed by.

1940: Rags, Casper McCullough's terrier, made John Hix' Strange as it Seems, for his feat of fetching golf-balls. He never touched a ball in play.

town turned out to see the first ground landing ever witnessed in Banff. Goodman, who at the time was working with Béla Bartók and József Szigeti on Bartók's "Contrasts for Piano, Violin, and Clarinet," got his trip and Banff got its landing strip.

Goodman was only one of a great number of celebrities to visit the hotel during the golden years. Jack Benny used American silver dollars for tips around the hotel, which was about the best type of tip available in those days (although most recipients would agree that the chauffeur who was once given $150 Canadian to drive a party into Calgary took top prize in the tip department); and Mickey Rooney, then involved in the Andy Hardy series, was turned down by some unsuspecting debutante when he asked her to dance. Cole Porter, Gracie Fields, Henry Fonda—the list is endless—were other well-known names who found time to spend a day or a week at the hotel.

Ginger Rogers sketching a Stony Chief.

The thirties were the hey-day of press-agentry, that particularly zany (and successful) type of promotion which saw starlets sitting on blocks of ice during hot weather or attempting to drive a golf ball with a 25-foot club while standing on the back of an elephant. The idea was to provide such an offbeat or topical photograph that the major news services would run the picture, thus advertising either the personality or the place which desired the publicity. In the case of the Banff Springs Hotel the personality and the place usually worked together, and one discovers photographs of the late Tommie Tweed, a well-known radio actor and dramatist, playing the Banff Springs golf course while dressed in a suit of armour, and Ginger Rogers sitting prettily on a rock and sketching a Stony chieftan.

Such pictures were almost always valuable publicity, but it happened more than once that the shots were obtained at a certain social price. When Kate Smith arrived at the hotel in the late thirties, it was decided that she should have her picture taken with some of the Indians at the Morley Reserve. They were given special instructions not to mention Miss Smith's physical proportions, which were only slightly less grand than the size of her infinitely expanding heart. On the drive to Morley the entertainer revealed that she was an honorary Iroquois princess and the accompanying photographer, Nick Morant, decided she should be dressed as a squaw for the shot. Upon arriving at Morley, Nick introduced Kate to the Indians and then inquired about a squaw outfit. Jacob Twoyoungman, the chief, hesitated a moment, looked up at the sky, and then said, "Jesus, Nick, I'm sorry—no squaws that big!"

The motion picture industry also provided some publicity for the hotel when it was decided that the building would be the backdrop for the dramatic capture of three escaped Nazis in the filming of *The Forty-Ninth Parallel*, an anti-German effort which somehow managed to plunk several of the Führer's disciples into the middle of the Bow River.

Yet another sort of publicity was gained for the hotel and the Banff environs when James Ramsey Ullman, the well-known writer of mountaineering tales, spent his first honeymoon at the hotel in 1927. A certain amount of his stay was devoted to climbing the peaks near Lake Louise with Rudolph Aemmer, one of the Swiss guides in the area, and from his experiences with Aemmer he wrote *The White Tower*.[4]

The most entertaining moments at the hotel didn't always involve the well-known entertainment celebrities. A particular Maharaja, it seems, arrived at the hotel one summer during the mid-thirties with a retinue of some 30 persons. He rented two or three of the larger suites and made clear his intentions of making his stay a lavish epic. The staff didn't blink a collective eye when he ordered two double beds together, but there was a certain amount of circulated amusement when it was discovered that the potentate was using the two beds solely for his own comfort and his various women were left to sleep on the floor.

[4]The first, and possibly only, direct fictional reference to the Banff Springs Hotel is in a 1908 novel, *Lady Merton, Colonist*, by Mrs. Humphrey Ward. It is a novel of romantic intrigue which interestingly uses as its major setting a trans-Canadian railway journey. The reference to the hotel is a rather flowery description of the view from the front balcony.

During the course of the Maharaja's visit it was discovered that the lock of the royal jewel box had become jammed and couldn't be opened. The hotel sent up one of the electricians, a man good with locks, to see if he could do anything to remedy the problem. The fellow found the box to be a most beautiful one, inlaid with gems and jewels, but he also found that the lock on the box was a very cheap one—the sort that can usually be opened with a bobby pin. Realizing that if he opened the box at once it would probably be taken away from him before he got a chance to peek inside, the amateur locksmith pretended to have difficulty with the lock, hoping that the assembled throng of onlookers would eventually lose interest and drift away. The ploy worked and he found himself alone with the box. Quickly opening the lock he lifted the lid and peered inside. The contents, he swears to this day, were somewhat less than he expected: at the bottom of the beautifully finished little container lay a single rumpled copy of the Calcutta racing news.

Another distinguished and frequent visitor was the Prince of Wales, later Edward VIII. The Prince was particularly fond of Alberta—so much so, in fact, that he bought a ranch some miles south of Calgary and would spend as much time as possible there each year. He also spent a fair amount of time in Banff and the mountainous environs, and it is rumoured each local girl knew somewhere in her heart of hearts she was the proper woman for the royal bachelor. But, alas, it was a matter of royal blood, and royal blood was in short supply in the villages of the Canadian Rockies. It was under the Prince's patronage that the Highland Gathering was held each year.

In May of 1939 King George VI and Queen Elizabeth stopped off at Banff on their transcontinental tour. Canada's prime minister, William Lyon Mackenzie King, was with them, filling out the most awesome political triumvirate ever to visit the hotel. The King and Queen and retinue had the entire hotel to themselves for two days, and the management was able to concentrate its considerable administrative abilities on the couple. One of the special touches featured by the hotel for their visit was the distribution of huge bou-

H.R.H. Prince of Wales

King George VI, Queen Elizabeth and Prime Minister William Lyon Mackenzie King visit the Banff Springs Hotel, 1939.

quets of wildflowers throughout the building, something the Queen took special note of.

The couple proved to be as genteel as the royal tradition requires, and gracefully consented to stop in and have tea at the home of their Banff chauffeur, Jim Brewster. It is a matter of some local historical humour that Jim failed to notify his wife he was bringing the King and Queen.

There were other, more earthy, guests. Most of the staff who worked at the hotel through the thirties remembers a certain Miss Steele, an old spinster who was perhaps more eccentric even than the Maharaja but who didn't rate the social insularity provided by a foreign birth. Miss Steele used to arrive at the hotel every summer with yards and yards of two-inch medical tape with which she would promptly seal off all the windows and doors to her room. This was evidently to prevent any stray wisp of smoke from drifting into her room. Cigarette smokers, she was sure, were trying to poison her. In the dining room she would take her meals in a distant corner and if anyone who had the slightest appearance of being a smoker chose to sit at an adjoining table she would immediately gather her eating appurtenances together and move to some other distant corner. Although quite wealthy, she made a habit of wearing an old brown coat around the hotel which, to put it mildly, was quite sat out. She finally joined the Banff Springs Hall of Infamy one summer by leaving a small bag of candies as a tip for the girl who had looked after her hermetically sealed room all season. "But I wouldn't eat them, dear," she told the girl, presenting her with the rumpled brown paper bag, "I think they've got worms in them."

Luckier than the young housekeeper was one of the drivers for the Brewster Company, the local transport outfit that has enjoyed a long and close relationship with the hotel. As a Brewster driver, the young man was hired by one of the hotel guests, a middle-aged and wealthy woman, to be her personal chauffeur for the summer. The woman became quite fond of the driver and at the season's end asked him if he wouldn't drive her to her home in San Francisco. The fellow acquiesced and the two of them left for California. At the trip's end she reluctantly said good-bye and presented him with a token of her esteem—a cheque made out for $1500, a sum, she said, which was to go toward his college education.

The hotel managed to deal with the idiosyncrasies of wealth in good fashion. When a Doctor Fowler from New York demanded that he be provided with fresh goat's milk at mealtime, a goat was bought and tethered at the back of the hotel and one of the busboys was appointed the official milker. Dear Miss Steele thought she might freeze to death in her surgically bound room and the hotel installed an extra length of radiator in her bathroom. And it was taken as a matter of fact (and usually interest) that every Saturday night someone would try on the suit of armour that used to stand at the bottom of the staircase near the ballroom[5]—the staff became quite habituated to the sound of an

[5]The same suit of armour now presides over the Black Knight Lounge in the Royal York Hotel in Toronto.

Tea in the conservatory.

errant knight in his cups ricocheting down the dimly lit corridors.

The staff itself in those days was a strictly professional outfit, and the same people who worked the Banff Springs in the summer would spend the winters at the great resorts in California, Hawaii, Bermuda, and Florida.[6] As might be expected with professionals, the staff was highly efficient (although they might have denied it at the time) and, as the depression wore on, increasingly dedicated to their jobs.

One of the best-remembered of the golden years' staff was a diminutive but charming maitre d' named Oscar Wulliman, a man seemingly pre-destined to serve the calling of the great dining rooms of the

[6]Changing labour laws and the later years of the depression eventually settled most of the seasonal professionals at year-round resorts. The Japanese bellboys received the *coup de grâce* upon the outbreak of the Sino-Japanese War in 1935. Today much of the summer staff is drawn from the ranks of university students.

continent. He did, in fact, prove to be such an excellent servant that the King of Siam insisted that Oscar accompany him as his personal waiter to Victoria, and then he tried to engage him on a permanent basis. Wulliman, however, declined the offer and returned to Banff.

Oscar's dedication to the hotel and to the cause of elegant dining was demonstrated more fully at a later date when he was serving a private dinner party for the visiting Reynolds (of Reynolds Tobacco fame) family. Mr. Reynolds had caught a prize trout and, in the usual hotel tradition, it was exhibited during the day in the hotel lobby. That night the fish was stuffed, garnished, and baked to order and Wulliman entered the dining room with the fish held high on a silver platter. But, as fate would have it, someone had dropped a pat of butter on one of the two steps which lead into the room and, as happens once in every waiter's life, Wulliman and the fish went down together. To the not-so-dulcet sound of some not-so-polite snickers, Oscar pieced the fish together and proceeded to the Reynold's table where he served the meal as best he could with one arm—the other had been broken in the fall!

Another well-remembered staff member is a chef named Robert. Robert was as evil-tempered and spiteful as Oscar was polite and charming. In the true chef's tradition he threw pots and pans around the kitchen, hurled carving knives at helpers, and, one day, reaped all that he had sown. Walking past the still room (the area where the specialty items, such as fancy desserts, are prepared) one evening toward the end of the season, Robert made some passing comment to a young female helper who was doing something on the far side of a long counter which ran the length of the room. The girl made some flippant reply (the exact nature of the conversation is now long lost) and Robert exploded. Brandishing a large spoon he leapt into the room and vaulted over the top of the counter —to land with great ceremony right in the middle of 360 dessert dishes of jello, each topped with whipped cream and one-quarter of a maraschino cherry.

There were also, upon occasion, certain administrative mishaps. An over-anxious front desk clerk one year managed to check the first two parties of the

Wᴴᴱʀᴇ have they been all day, these butterfly ladies who flutter around the hotel at night in Paris gowns? Riding the trails and roaming the forests in strictly utilitarian togs. After sundown they revert to type, chattering over Banff's smart frocks, whispering over newly met "hims," in this purely feminine retreat. Women especially delight in Banff's refinements of service, its exquisite linens and china, finer than in many wealthy homes. Another purely feminine joy is the beauty parlor where some of the smartest women in the world are skilfully attended.

season into the same room, a *faux pas* known in the trade as "double-rooming." And at the end of the same year, after the staff had carefully checked out the last of the guests, someone discovered a fellow sleeping soundly in a laundry room, the victim of certain excesses indulged in at the hotel's closing ceremony the night before. He had been overlooked in the general rush to close the hotel.

Despite such occurrences, however, the hotel did well manage to maintain its atmosphere of cultured decorum. Proper dress for the evening concerts and dances was full formal attire, and no one would dare approach the dining room without a tie and jacket. No less a personage than Lady Duff Cooper was refused entrance to the Alhambra when she appeared at the door one day in her blue jeans, just back from a long trip on the trail.

There was one spot, though, where Lady Cooper would have been more than welcome in whatever she chose to wear. There was, where the hotel's parking lot is today, a small Chinese restaurant known as Sam's Place. It was officially a restaurant for Brewster packers and drivers, but unofficially it served as a common meeting ground for not only Brewster cowboys but hotel staff and guests as well. It became, in time, as much a part of the hotel experience as the evening dance.

Sam's was known as *the place* for anyone interested in having a good meal and a good time after the hotel's kitchens closed for the evening, and 11 p.m. on any given summer's evening would find the small building packed with a wide and interesting assortment of folks. Cowboys well into their cups could go through their routines with an eye on the brunette debutante in the corner, and the suave young men in tuxedos could at last put their elbows on the counter and talk to the chambermaids. Sam's Place still occupies a special position in the hearts of hotel staff and guests of the mid-thirties.

By 1940 the impact of World War Two was being felt throughout Canada, and Banff, as a resort town, equated its well-being with the well-being of the nation. For the Banff Springs Hotel the war meant the loss of its European patronage, and restrictions on money and travel hindered North American travel as

Sam's Place — always a little bit informal.

well. By 1942 it was decided that the hotel would close its doors for the duration of the war.

With the closing of the doors came the closing of the greatest era in the hotel's history, an era rich in the counterpoint of stiff Victorian propriety and that new sort of life which saw young women protesting a bit too much as young men dragged them toward the pool. The grand halls, now empty, echoed not only the soothing strains of a Mozart trio but the sound of the eternal drunk in the knight's outfit as well. The life of great glitter was over, perhaps never to be recaptured in quite the same spirit.

X

Tribulations and Triumph
The Transition Decades

"a grand old hotel looking at the 2lst century"

The altered world that emerged from World War II brought significant change to the Banff Springs Hotel. Though the passing years have done little to diminish the castle's initial impact on its visitors, a rapidly evolving economic and social climate has created a much different hotel than that which opened its doors in the late nineteenth century.

The most obvious change — the full "democratization" of the Banff Springs — had in fact begun just prior to its wartime closing in 1942, as the hotel began to cater to large numbers of regularly scheduled package train tours. Attractively affordable, the tours orginiated in the East but followed a western itinerary that commonly included a night or two in Banff at the Banff Springs Hotel. The trips became popular quickly, and in a few short years the middle–class clientèle they appealed to was threatening to replace the well–heeled, long-term guests as the hotel's "ruling class."

The expansion of the hotel's social base was completed by the Second World War and the accompanying North American economic boom. Suddenly, it seemed, everyone in America had a car and the money to put gas in it. There were more and better roads to drive, and many of them, it seemed, led to Banff — a state of affairs that led one weary victim of too many resort summers to reason that, "Fortunately, just as many of them lead away."

To be sure, a lot of the old clientèle still spent their summers at the Banff Springs and the Château Lake Louise, and the list of celebrities continued to grow — many visitors from that era remember the bellboys arguing as to which of them would push Marilyn Monroe in her wheelchair after she twisted her ankle filming *River of No Return*[1] — but each year a higher percentage of the hotel's total earnings came from short-stay, tour-scheduled tourists.

In keeping with the times and the desires of its guests, the hotel began to relax its customs of formality. Dress for concert and dance slipped from formal to semi-formal and the occasional gentleman could be found in the dining room *sans* tie. Other of the old traditions lingered gracefully on, however; indeed, the hotel administration worked overtime to popularize some of them. In the early post-war years a radio broadcast room was installed in one of the hotel towers and for years thereafter people across Canada tuned in nightly to the big band arrangements of Mart Kenney or Moxie Whitney. The introduction to the programme never varied: "From the spacious ballroom of the Banff Springs Hotel, situated mile-high in the Canadian Rockies . . ."

Slowly, however, as the 1950s became the 1960s,

---

[1] Marilyn is falsely rumoured to have followed a precedent set some years earlier by another star — Lassie — by going over the Bow Falls in the service of her art. As a matter of interest, Lassie, in town to shoot *Lassie Come Home*, was probably the first dog openly welcome at the hotel. In later years, Alan Ladd had to smuggle his cocker spaniel in and out a back door, and another guest, a Mrs. Sifton, was told she could not bring her lap dog into the hotel — a refusal that prompted her to break off all relations with the CPR and hire a taxi to take her to San Francisco.

the hotel's golden gilding began to wear thin. The days of the private coach on the mainline were as dead as the old six-horse tallyho; the hotel was catering almost exclusively to conventions, bus tours, and automobile-oriented families; and the CPR, which had become a diversified corporation, was much less concerned with its hotels than in Van Horne's day. Money for maintenance and renovations became scarce, and managers were appointed as much on the basis of company service as working knowledge of hotels. Little by little, the Banff Springs began to show its age: paint peeled, plaster crumbled, and bedspreads frayed; the plumbing and wiring became obsolete. In contrast to the sleek, spacious rooms offered by younger, more aggressive international chains, those at the Banff Springs suddenly appeared cramped and dingy. The sole bright spot in the whole of the 1960s, it seemed, came in 1969, when the hotel fulfilled the dream of earlier management by remaining open for the winter season. The halls were drafty and occasionally downright cold, but with an après-ski lounge, rock bands, and a young crowd vying for attention with all the vigour of those ladies in their ridicule-defying outfits of 1925, the Banff Springs let it be known it was not yet ready to yield its position of prominence to the hotels downtown. Banff itself had at long last become a year-round resort.

The hotel required an immense amount of work — at least one guest in that winter of 1969 ranked his accommodation on a par with his old college dorm room — and it needed someone to take up its cause. Fortunately, it found such a champion in Ivor Petrak, a former CPR employee who returned to the company to become hotel manager in 1971. Petrak brought to the hotel not only a solid background in hotel management but, even more critically, a sensitivity to the Banff Springs' history and a determination to restore the hotel to its former grandeur, though in a contemporary context. "Van Horne had the vision," Petrak is fond of saying, "I had the mission."

Accordingly, he went to work, not only on the hotel but on the CPR board of directors, convincing them to recommit the company to the old standards of excellence. Petrak's own commitment was total: In his first year, he began reworking the hotel from top to bottom. Step one was to repaint and refurnish 75 rooms on the ninth floor and create a new suite, also on the ninth floor, from some rooms previously used for furniture storage. The following year, catering to his winter guests, he converted the old Garden View Lounge into a warm, intimate dining club and lounge called the Rob Roy, and put in a new cabaret in the downstairs arcade. Thereafter, he redid 150 rooms a year — carpentry, painting, bedspreads, upholstery — drawing heavily on the sensibilities and inspiration of Lazlo Funtek, a respected theatre set designer from the Banff Centre. In 1975 he rewired the hotel and elevator, a $20 million job, and three years later updated the plumbing for another $15 million. He also reworked the arcade floor a second time, creating space for a number of small shops, boutiques and restaurants, and he continued to convert unused space to imaginative new rooms and suites. One three-floor suite, for instance, was fashioned from a housekeeper's apartment, which in turn had been built around one of the old hotel staircases. In its current configuration, a small pine-clad nook and bar on the first floor gives way to a gracious set of stairs that climbs to a wide landing, out of which a small living area and bedchamber have been fashioned. From the landing, the stairs, six-feet wide and 14 in number, double back and sweep majestically up to the bathroom, which, to its credit, features a large jacuzzi bath and bidet. One of its

occupants, mishearing a bellboy caution him about the flight of stairs, soon had the hotel staff in stitches by his proud references to his being booked in the "Fred Astaire" suite.

Those renovations, however, were only Petrak's opening salvo. In the fall of 1980, having been through the hotel once to ensure the hotel's service infrastructure was modern and its accommodation "adequate," he launched a new campaign to bring all the rooms and public spaces closer to the standard he sought. This time around, the instructions were that each room receive individual attention and detailing, with no one design being repeated more than three times in the entire hotel. The outside swimming pool was also rebuilt for four seasons: in the winter, when air temperatures hover well below zero, it becomes a welcoming, steaming hot pool for weary skiers. Yet another restaurant was brought into the hotel, and Petrak's passion for turning old corners into new rooms continued unabated. He began to enclose some exterior balconies and odd outside crannies, creating in the process unique public spaces like the Van Horne Room and private rooms like the ground floor Admiral's Suite. Uniformly, their greatest attraction is their interior feature walls of the old Rundle limestone.

By 1982, more than $60 million had gone into the hotel, and still Petrak showed no sign of slowing down. As early as 1976, Parks Canada had approved an elaborate, two-phase programme that would change both the hotel and its grounds, but it wasn't until after a number of political and financial obstacles had been cleared in 1985 that the hotel was able to begin the project. Phase I, with a budget of $37.5 million, saw the conversion of the old staff building called the Annex into a new 250-room guest wing called the Manor; the construction of 336 new staff apartments (which, according to Petrak, "provide the best staff accommodation in the world") and 35 townhouses for senior staff on land just west of the hotel; and the addition of a new clubhouse and nine new golf holes, designed by master course architect Geoffrey Cornish to the existing golf facilities.[1] With the exception of the golf course improvements, the Phase I work was completed in time for the 1988 centennial celebrations. In the hotel proper, cozy little two-floor honeymoon suites complete with spiral stairs, heartshaped headboards and jacuzzis were tucked into the uppermost tower turrets, and the hotel's most luxurious suite, the President's, was fashioned from rooms on the 10th floor and empty space on the 11th and 12th floors. Opened in December of 1986, the suite features marble, brass and plush fabrics throughout, an exterior glass elevator to transport guests from floor to floor, eight bedrooms with canopied beds and ornate original wall tapestries, a reception foyer and fireplace, private concierge service, and a multilevel living room with baby grand piano, loft library, stereo system and 50-inch television set. There is a sauna, jacuzzi bath, lap pool and, notably, a toilet wedged into a little corner of one of the bathrooms that offers those who use it a glorious, unimpeded overlook of the confluence of the Bow and Spray Rivers — the old "million dollar view." Because of the awkward configuration of the turret corner in

[1]Which are not inconsiderable. *Golf Digest* magazine once rated the original 18 Stanley Thompson holes as among the top ten in the world. Local rules have it that the 40,000 golfers who annually tour the links shall *not* be penalized for golf balls eaten by grizzlies.

Several of the new suites, including the Admiral's Suite, incorporate the old exterior wall in their design.

which it sits, the toilet took carpenters and plumbers nearly three days to install, but the prospect from its seat alone nearly justifies the suite's price: $3,000 a night.

There is no shortage of guests who can afford the President's Suite. With the almost continual renovations of the last two decades, the number of royalty, politicians and celebrities visiting the hotel is now as high as it ever was. The list of names in recent memory includes Prime Ministers Trudeau, Clark and Mulroney, Lord Mountbatten, Prince Philip, Princess Alexandria, the Duke and Duchess of Kent, Indira Ghandi, Prince Norihito and Princess Takamatsu of Japan, Prince Rainier, Arnold Schwarzenegger and Marie Shriver, Jack Lemmon, Lee Marvin, Margot Kidder, and Brooke Shields.

And, as in the past, the presence of celebrities continues to add to the store of hotel anecdotes. When Prince Bernhardt of the Netherlands stayed at the hotel in October of 1972, he entered an elevator one day to be confronted by a chipper, chatty and obviously unwitting elevator attendant. After exchanging greetings and pleasantries about the weather, the young woman smiled at the Prince and asked, "And what do you do when you're not staying with us?"

In the year of the hotel's centenary, musician Louis Trono had been playing for Banff Spring guests for 65 years.

"Actually," replied a bemused Prince Bernhardt, "I'm a prince."

"All right!" said the young lady, extending her hand. "And I'm the Queen of England. Pleased to meet you."

Although renovation has encouraged the rich and famous to visit the hotel once again, modernization has evidently done little to dispel the notion of the hotel as a haunted castle. Elegant ghosts in formal evening dress are rumoured to make occasional appearances in the Rob Roy, with the wrinkle that they appear only from the waist up. The floor of the new lounge was constructed some three feet above the original and it appears the ghosts still stalk the old level. There is also a story about some guests who returned to their room one night to find the lock to their door jammed. They called down to the bell desk for help, but when the bell boy arrived, he found the party sitting comfortably in their room. They thanked him for coming up, but said they had already been assisted by an elderly man in a uniform different from that worn by the bell boys. Their description was of a deceased bell captain who had often said that, given the chance, he would like to come back to the hotel as a ghost once he had passed on.

An architect's rendering of the Banff Springs, showing the planned entertainment and shopping complex and Van Horne gardens.

      With or without ghosts, however, it is apparent that in the year of its centennial the Banff Springs has come a long way toward regaining its former stature, blending architectural and historic charm with state-of-the-art appointments and facilities. It is, once again, on a par with any hotel on the continent. Future plans, such as the Phase II construction of a major entertainment and shopping centre, are as grandiose as any in its history. The facility will be built where the old bus garage now stands and will include a 400-seat auditorium, a six-lane bowling alley, a movie theatre, a western-style bar, and a shopping arcade connecting it to the Manor. There will also be a new garden, at the centre of which will stand a statue of William Cornelius Van Horne. Although he will overlook a creation that might now impress him in the way the original hotel surprised old Morley Roberts, there is little doubt Van Horne would recognize it with approval: a sumptuous castle in the wilderness, welcoming in style travelers from all over the world.

XI

Day After Day

"Intricate as a clock, the hotel moves into its future"

As the Banff Springs Hotel enters its second century, one might think it ready to slide into the role of the grand old character of the mountains — settle back on its laurels and impress the youngsters with tales of the good old days, when the wilderness still had some wild in it. In the hostelry business, however — as the CPR was reminded in the 1960s — age is a relative state and neither fabled past, grand architecture nor wondrous setting guarantees the future. Those elements help immensely, of course, but are ultimately only part of a larger package that includes last week's decor, yesterday's service and the taste of this morning's coffee. Thus, even with the celebration of its 100th birthday in 1988, the hotel remains a dynamic, vigorous institution, as dedicated as ever to Van Horne's admonishment that if something is not moving full speed ahead, it is moving backwards.

Administering such an operation is a challenging job, and its day-to-day operation is made even more so in that, if successful, it is all but invisible to the guests

enjoying it. At even the best of times, however, when most visitors are aware only of their own pleasure in the hotel and its particular ambience, there are always some who are interested in just how the hotel handles the multitude of tasks required for its successful operation. Once they begin to investigate the behind-the-scenes running of the place, they discover a realm nearly as interesting as the hotel's architecture and history.

Obviously, it takes large numbers of people and large amounts of capital to maintain large buildings — especially if the building's business is catering to still larger numbers of people. In 1930, after the major construction on the hotel had been completed, it was estimated that the CPR had spent some nine million dollars on the property since 1887, and by the early 1970s it was thought it might take as much as $50 million to reconstruct the Banff Springs from scratch — granting that someone could be found who could handle the work. Today, following the CPR's recommitment to the hotel and its multi-million dollar investment of the past 20 years, no one will hazard a guess as to the cost of recreating the Banff Springs. Its total worth, however, is somewhere in the quarter of a billion dollar range. The scale of its operation is reflected in the fact that it takes in the neighbourhood of $80,000 day simply to keep its doors open.

Much of that daily overhead goes toward paying the salaries of the hotel staff which, in the peak months, numbers about 1,000 people. A rough breakdown of the figure shows 250 in housekeeping, 550 in food and beverages, 80 in grounds and maintenance (including 30 for the golf course), and close to 55 in administration. There are 15 security guards, 14 parking attendants, eight telephone operators, six recreation and sports specialists, and a staff of 35 just to look after the rest of the staff.

The number of hotel guests is nearly as impressive as the number of staff; with the opening of the Manor in 1988, the Banff Springs can accommodate upward of 1750 guests at one time. The actual occupancy is 100 per cent six months each year, and runs at between 82 and 90 per cent year round — not a bad figure in an industry that averages just over 70 per cent. Given that the hotel experiences a complete visitor turn-over up to three times a week, the actual annual number of guests, in excess of 200,000, is astonishing. And it would be even higher, except that the hotel restricts its occupancy to 50 per cent during the weekdays between October 20th and December 20th each year to provide the time and space necessary for repair and maintenance.

There are 828 bedrooms in the hotel, and another 13 meeting rooms that are converted to bedrooms in the summer. Many of the rooms link together to form the hotel's 66 suites, 25 of which feature jacuzzi baths. Depending on the season and the room, guests will pay from $65 to $175 for a single room, $70 to $195 for a double, and anywhere from $195 to $3,000 for a suite.

Guest services are extensive; the hotel, in fact, nearly becomes a self-contained city during the summer months. The range of services includes a post office, currency exchange, full laundry with dry cleaning, barber shop and beauty parlour, newstand, rent-a-car outlet, photography service, flower shop, variety of gift boutiques and, seasonally, retail and rental shops for golf, tennis and skiing.

In a recreational vein, the hotel today carries on the traditions of the past while expanding the list of available activities to include a few peculiar to the late twentieth century. The hotel itself features two pools, a sauna, whirlpool, rooftop jacuzzi, health club, weight room and tanning beds. There is tennis, golf, shuffleboard, ice skating, croquet, badminton, volleyball, basketball, and a field for soccer and baseball, and, for anyone overdoing any of the above, a licensed masseuse. There are also a number of hotel concessions that coordinate off-property activities: hiking, climbing, horseback riding, river rafting, canoeing, fishing, wind surfing, bicycling and downhill, cross-country and helicopter skiing. For the more sedentary there are winter sleigh rides and year round sightseeing tours. And, lest the night owls be left out, a fullblown nightclub and bar, the Works, in the hotel arcade.

The hotel's food and beverage operation offers another interesting area of investigation. All food and drink for the hotel's eight restaurants (ranging from formal dining rooms like the Alhambra to such specialty spots as the Samurai Sushi Bar and the Espresso Cafe), and four bars are coordinated through the hotel food and beverage office. The responsibility is no small one: in 1987, the year *before* the new 250-room Manor guest wing opened, the hotel purchased some $4.5 million worth of food for its 80 chefs to prepare in their various kitchens. Visitors consumed more than 88,000 pounds of their favourite entrée, prime rib, almost 40,000 pounds of striploins, 3,000 pounds of lamb racks, an astonishing 44,000 pounds of premium bacon, 47,000 dozen eggs,

and 150,000 quarts of milk. Among the various speciality food items the hotel offers, the most popular is sockeye salmon; in 1987, guests ate some 20,000 pounds, much of which was flown in fresh during the summer.

The alcoholic drinks imbibed in a year are equally impressive. Again in 1987, the hotel's gross beverage purchase came to $1.3 million. Of that total, hard liquor constituted 28 per cent, wine 39 per cent, beer 21 per cent, and minerals 12 per cent. To put the figures in perspective, the beer — 300,000 bottles — was enough to fill an Olympic swimming pool. As might be expected, the popularity of mixed drinks varies with the season, but across any given year vodka and rye are steadfastly the two biggest sellers.

In recent years, most of the guests who have packed away such prodigious quantities of food and liquor have come from two sources: conventions (including company incentive programmes) and tours. The hotel schedules most of its convention business through the spring and fall, but leaves the peak months of July and August open for tour bookings, which constitute over 80 per cent of its business during those months. The hotel deals with over 50 different touring companies, most of which run a continuing series of trips through the Rockies throughout the summer months. Most tours spend one or two nights at the hotel, operating on the modified American plan of room and two meals a day. During the winter, special chartered "ski-week" packages account for much of the hotel's business.

In the past, conventions were primarily booked for June, September and October, but in more recent years the hotel has extended the convention season to include the early spring and most of the winter. In May of 1988, the hotel hosted 34 conventions alone, and in the course of any given year will entertain well over 200. The largest such gathering in the hotel's history, however, dates the 1971 Canadian Bar Association convention, a meeting of around 2,400 persons that the hotel handled in conjunction with the Banff Centre. For the final banquet, the Banff Springs dined close to 1,500 of the lawyers. Closed circuit television kept the head table at the hotel in touch with the head table at the Banff Centre, where the remaining conventioneers were eating.

The hotel further caters to private functions such as parties, business luncheons and weddings. During the summer, there will be on average one wedding a day at the hotel, most commonly taking place in the conservatory.

Despite its longstanding reputation, the hotel cannot sit back passively and wait for business to come its way. Although most of the tours and conventions represent repeat business, the hotel management actively courts new sources of clientèle. The Banff Springs, in conjunction with the other mountain CPR properties, is sold through various regional offices (major centres include New York, Chicago, Washington D.C., Los Angeles and Dallas, as well as Toronto and Vancouver), whose representatives directly approach convention possibilities — companies that hold annual meetings or have incentives programmes for the employees, for example, or organizations that sponsor major exhibits or trade shows.

Similarly, the hotel sells itself abroad. The hotel has a sales office in London, and representatives from

four or five CPR hotels regularly tour Japan, Europe, Australia and Hong Kong, extending to executives and travel agents an invitation to come and see for themselves what the different institutions have to offer in the way of tourist and convention facilities.

The running of the hotel, then, is no simple matter. Problems with guests, staff, the physical plant, and the head office arise each day and must be dealt with quickly and efficiently for the hotel's successful operation. Intricate as the workings of the four Black Forest grandfather clocks in its lobbies — clocks which have never had to be reset in 50 years of service — the hotel moves minute by minute into its future.

Appendix:
Periods and Pieces

Many present-day visitors to the Banff Springs Hotel find the general decor and furnishing of the building provide a rich and exciting area for investigation. Compiled here are some data which might help answer the questions of such interested guests.

ARCHITECTURAL PERIODS

Mount Stephen Hall. The Mount Stephen Hall is one of the great halls of the North American continent. It is representative of 15th century Gothic architecture and was named for Lord Mount Stephen, first President of the CPR. Notable features include the floor of Bedford lime flagstones, the stained-glass crests in the windows (see Crests, below), and the great oak ceiling beams which feature crests of the Provinces of Alberta, British Columbia, Manitoba, New Brunswick, Nova Scotia, Ontario, Prince Edward Island, Quebec, and Saskatchewan. Newfoundland was not a province at the time the hall was built.

The Oak Room. The Oak Room, which adjoins Mount Stephen Hall, also evidences Gothic influence and is noted for its panelled walls and linenfold carvings.

The Strathcona and Angus Rooms. Both the Strathcona and Angus Rooms, private dining rooms just off the Alhambra Dining Room, are in the Norman Gothic style.

The Alhambra Dining Room. The Alhambra Dining Room shows strong Spanish Renaissance influence. Particularly notable are the cast bronze doors which guard the entrance to the room and the plaque of the Santa Maria above the fireplace in the foyer. The circular staircase which leads off the foyer offers a good example of the fossiliferous Tyndall stone. The ceiling to the stairway exhibits some beautiful "mushroom" plasterwork, while the stairway itself is lighted by irreplaceable Tiffany lamps.

Library. The Library features oak walls panelled in the Tudor style.

Private Suites. A number of the hotel's 66 suites showcase a particular period motif and/or national style. Among those available are suites featuring the following influences:

Jacobean and Stuart
Tudor (showing Elizabethan and Jacobean influence)
Italian
Swiss
Georgian
Empire
Louis XV

FURNITURE

The furniture pieces in the public spaces of the hotel represent many periods and many styles. A partial listing of the pieces includes:
Chairs:

Gothic chairs, courting chairs, and love seats
Small Princess Mary chairs
Queen Anne wing chairs
Italian folding chairs
English chair-tables
Spanish torcheres
Jacobean hall seats

Cupboards and Sideboards:

Gothic cupboard
Flemish cupboard
Tudor style sideboard
Elizabethan style sideboard

Elizabethan refectory table
English writing desks
English chair-table

CRESTS

Speculation often runs high concerning the crests and mottoes found in the Mount Stephen Hall and the Oak Room. Below is a compilation of the mottoes, their translation, and the CPR officials to whom they belonged:

Mount Stephen Hall:

Contra Audentior, In Opposition More Daring, Lord Mount Stephen

Modestia et Fidelitas, Modest and Loyal, Sir Edward Beatty

A Mari Usque Ad Mare, From Sea to Sea, Dominion of Canada

Manu Forti, With a Strong Hand, Lord Thomas Shaughnessy

Nil Desperandum, Never Despairing, Sir William Van Horne

Semper Eadem, Always the Same, J. M. R. Fairbairn

Solus Christus Mea Rupes, Christ Alone is my Rock, J. W. Orrock

Omnia Vincit Amor, Love Conquers All Things, Miss Kate Treleaven

A Cuspide Corona, From the Spear a Crown, M. P. Delahanty

The Oak Room:

Callide Et Honeste, With Skill and Honour, W. Wainright

Fidem Servo, I Keep Faith, E. Alexander

Ne Vele Veles, Form No Vile Wish, C. E. E. Ussher

Fortitudine, With Fortitude, A. Allerton

Serviendo Guberno, I Govern by Serving, J. J. Scully

Nec Temere, Nec Timide, Neither Rashly nor Timidly, W. M. Neal

Bibliography

Books

The Countess of Aberdeen. *Through Canada with a Kodak.* Edinburgh: W. H. White and Co. 1892.

Baedeker, Karl. *The Dominion of Canada: Handbook for Travellers.* New York: Charles Scribner's Sons. 1907.

Bell, Archie. *Sunset Canada.* Boston: Colonial Press, 1918.

Campbell, Robert. *I Would do it Again.* Toronto: Ryerson Press, 1959.

Dewar, Thomas R. *A Ramble Round the Globe.* London: Chatto and Windus, 1894.

Fear, G. M. *Banff and Its Beauties.* Toronto: MacFarlane. (before 1900.)

Fraser, John Foster. *Canada As It Is.* London: Cassell and Company, 1905.

Gibbon, John Murray. *Steel of Empire: The Romantic History of the Canadian Pacific.* Toronto: McClelland & Stewart, 1935.

Gowans, Alan. *Building Canada: An Architectural History of Canadian Life.* Toronto: Oxford University Press, 1966.

Ingersoll, Ernest. *The Canadian Guidebook* (Part II). London: William Heinemann, 1892.

Kalman H. D. *The Railway Hotels and the Development of the Chateau Style in Canada.* Victoria: The Maltwood Museum, 1968.

Luxton, N. K. *Fifty Switzerlands in One: Banff the Beautiful, Canada's National Park.* Banff, Luxton, 1923.

McEvoy, Bernard. *From the Great Lakes to the Wide West.* Toronto: William Briggs, 1902.

Morton, W. L., ed. *The Shield of Achilles.* Toronto: McClelland and Stewart Limited, 1968. (Particularly, Alan Gowans, "The Canadian National Style.")

Niven, Frederick, and W. J. Phillips. *Colour in the Canadian Rockies.* Toronto: Thomas Nelson and Sons, Ltd., 1937.

Roberts, Morley. *On the Old Trail* London: Eveleigh Nash and Grayson, Ltd., 1927.

Sladen, Douglas. *On the Cars and Off.* London: Ward, Lock, and Bowden, Ltd., 1895.

Somerset, Susan M. *Impressions of a Tenderfoot.* London: John Murray, 1896.

Vaugh, Walter. *The Life and Work of Sir William Van Horne.* New York: The Century Company, 1920.

Ward, Mrs. Humphrey. *Lady Merton, Colonist.* Toronto: The Musson Book Company, 1910.

Wilcox, Walter. *Camping in the Canadian Rockies.* New York: G. P. Putnam and Sons, 1897.

Articles, Periodicals, Pamphlets

Alberta Farmer, 1926.

Annual Reports of the Department of the Interior, 1902-1921.

The Architectural Record, June 1889. Great American Architects Series No. 5. A Review of the Works of Bruce Price.

Building, VI. February 26, 1887.

Calgary News Telegram, 1912-13.

Canadian Pacific Railway. *Banff Springs Hotel: In the Heart of the Canadian Rockies.*

—————. *The New Highway to the Orient.* Montreal: CPR, 1903.

—————. (Various promotional tracts and pamphlets, 1920-1950.)

Crag and Canyon, Banff, 1903-1973.

Dominion Illustrated, Vols. I, IV, 1888, 1890.

Edmonton Journal, 1972.

Rogatnik, Abraham. "Canadian Castles: Phenomena of the Railway Hotel," *Architectural Review*, CXLI (May, 1967).

Winnipeg Sun, 1887.

Unpublished Materials

Alice Fulmer. *The Old and a Touch of the New.* Archives of the Canadian Rockies, Banff.

Mrs. W. S. Painter. Tape interview. Archives of the Canadian Rockies, Banff.

Walter Painter. *Hotel floor plans.* Archives of the Canadian Rockies, Banff.

Dorothy Whyte. Personal correspondence.

Photo and Illustration Credits